Contents

Teena Kamen passed away suddenly on the 5th March 2013, shortly after completing this publication. As always, her family would like to dedicate this book to her son, Tom Jennings, with love and affection. They would also like to thank the children, families, students, colleagues and all the staff at Hodder Education who have known and worked with Teena over the years. Finally, they thank the author herself for her dedication to and love for not only her writing but her family and friends. We love and miss her very much.

Introduction

The new Early Years Foundation Stage (EYFS) framework makes clear that practitioners should observe and respond to each child in their care on an ongoing basis. It gives a broad steer that there should be a focus on the ***prime areas*** (personal, social and emotional development; physical development) for younger children, with gradual building in of support in the ***specific areas*** (literacy; mathematics; understanding the world; and expressive arts and design) for older age ranges, as appropriate to their individual progress and level of development. Experiences which support younger children's learning in the prime areas also support their learning in the specific areas; for example, sharing rhymes and picture books lays the foundations for reading and writing, as well as for developing communication and language.

This book clearly links theory and practice by exploring how you as a practitioner can use observation and assessment to consider the individual needs, interests, and stage of development of each child in your care, and how to use this information to plan a challenging and enjoyable experience for each child in all of the seven areas of learning and development.

This book explains complex issues (such as objectivity and ethics when observing young children) in ways which can easily be understood, but is sufficiently challenging to assist in developing a sound knowledge-base to complement your practical skills. This book examines the role of assessment in learning and teaching as well as explaining how to use effective assessment systems across the whole of the EYFS. There are clear instructions on how to carry out observations and collect on-going evidence of young children's development and learning, including how to involve the children and their parents in the assessment process. There is particular emphasis on the role of the early years practitioner in observing and assessing young children's learning and development including detailed information on:

- The process of using assessment to inform planning.
- Implementing an observation-based formative assessment system.
- The principles of child observation and assessment.
- The principles of record keeping and confidentiality.
- Observation methods and techniques.
- The summary of development at age 24 to 36 months.
- Assessment at the end of the EYFS – the Early Years Foundation Stage Profile.

This book also includes **activities** to develop the early years practitioner's personal and professional skills for observing and assessing young children in the EYFS and is linked to the new *Level 3 Diploma in Children and Young People's Workforce* (Early Years Pathway). This book is for students (and their tutors/assessors) on a variety of Level 3 early education and child care courses and provides easily accessible information for new and experienced practitioners working with children aged 0 to 5 years in a range of early years settings.

CHAPTER 1

An overview of observation and assessment in the context of the EYFS

This chapter provides you with an overview of observation and assessment within the context of the EYFS, including:

✻ The importance of observation

✻ The importance of assessment

✻ How observation and assessment in early years settings should be underpinned by the four guiding themes of the EYFS

✻ The assessment requirements of the EYFS.

Introduction

The Early Years Foundation Stage (EYFS) framework sets the standards for the learning, development and care of young children from birth to age 5. Since its introduction in September 2008, the EYFS has helped to improve outcomes for young children. The framework describes what good early years providers should do, the levels of development that most young children can be expected to reach by age 5, and the requirements against which Ofsted inspects, to ensure high quality. The framework supports an integrated approach to learning and care, with continuity for children for the transition from the foundation years into Year 1 of the National Curriculum. The updated EYFS framework took effect from September 2012 (DfE, 2011b).

On 6 July 2011 a revised draft EYFS framework was issued by the coalition government for consultation, taking forward Dame Clare Tickell's proposals for reform by:

- Reducing paperwork and bureaucracy for professionals.
- Focusing strongly on the three prime areas of learning that are most essential for young children's healthy development (Communication and Language; Physical Development; Personal, Social and Emotional Development), and focusing on future learning with four specific areas in which the prime areas are applied (Literacy; Mathematics; Understanding the World; Expressive Arts and Design).
- Simplifying assessment at age 5, including a reduction of the Early Learning Goals (ELGs) from 69 to 17.
- Providing for earlier intervention for those children who need extra help, through the introduction of a progress check when children are age 2.

(DfE, 2011b)

(There is more detailed information about the areas of learning in Chapter 5.)

Alongside the updated EYFS framework there are additional support materials, including:

- Guidance and exemplification for teachers on completing the Early Years Foundation Stage Profile.
- Best practice models for presenting information from the Progress Check at Age Two.
- A chart covering child development from birth to age 5 (covering both the prime and specific areas).
- A summary of the EYFS for parents.

(DfE, 2011b)

The importance of observation

Accurate observations and assessments form the foundations for all effective early years practice. To keep precise and useful records you need to know the young children you work with really well. Careful observations enable you and your colleagues to make objective assessments concerning young children and their individual:

- care needs
- behaviour patterns
- levels of development
- skills/abilities
- learning styles
- learning needs/goals
- learning achievements.

 Key Term

Behaviour: a person's actions, reactions and treatment of others.

Assessment of this information can help highlight and celebrate young children's strengths as well as identify any gaps in their learning. This information can form the basis for the ongoing planning of appropriate care routines, play opportunities and learning activities; it may also be a useful starting point for future learning goals/objectives.

Observations should cover all relevant aspects of child development, including:

- social development and behaviour
- physical skills
- intellectual abilities
- communication skills and language development
- emotional development.

The methods for recording observations depend on your setting's policies and any legal requirements (see below). (More information on observation methods and techniques can be found in Chapter 4.)

It is important to observe young children for many reasons, including:

- to understand the wide range of skills in all areas of young children's development
- to know and understand the sequence of young children's development
- to use this knowledge to link theory with your own practice in the setting
- to assess young children's development and existing skills or behaviour
- to plan care routines, play opportunities and learning activities appropriate to young children's individual developmental and learning needs.

A Activity

Why is it important to observe and assess young children's development and learning?

Assessment, reporting and planning

It is essential that all early years practitioners (in the maintained, independent, private and voluntary sectors) adopt the EYFS's principled approach to assessment, record keeping and demonstrating progress. The EYFS emphasises the importance of observational assessment as a key component of effective practice and as the means by which the next steps in young children's learning are identified. This includes understanding the requirements of both the EYFS and the setting with regard to assessment, reporting and planning. For example:

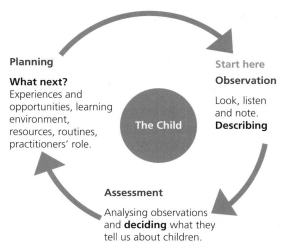

Figure 1.1 Observation, assessment and planning to support each child's development and learning (from Development Matters in the Early Years Foundation Stage, 2012, p.3)

- Dealing with issues relating to evidencing judgements.
- Developing approaches to manageable record keeping.
- Using data appropriately and demonstrating progress.

You should follow any guidance of what do to ensure that your practice in an early years setting is underpinned by the principles of assessment and the four key themes of the EYFS:

- A unique child
- Positive relationships
- A positive environment
- Learning and development.

(See section below, 'How observation and assessment in early years settings should be underpinned by the four guiding themes of the EYFS'.)

Legal requirement

Section 41 of the Childcare Act 2006 contains the duty to implement the Early Years Foundation Stage (EYFS), which is mandatory for the following providers:

- Providers registered on the Early Years Register (maintained by Ofsted).
- Providers exempt from registration on the Early Years Register in relation to provision for children aged 3 and older, where the provision is part of the school's activities, is provided by the school proprietor or their employee, and at least one child is a registered pupil at the school. This includes maintained schools, independent schools and non-maintained special schools.

(DfE, 2011b)

The Childcare Act 2006 requires the Secretary of State to specify learning and development requirements and welfare requirements. The learning and development requirements are given legal force by an order made under Section 39(1)(a) of the Childcare Act 2006. The safeguarding and welfare requirements are given legal force by regulations made under Section 39(1)(b) of the Childcare Act 2006. Together, the order, the regulations and the Statutory Framework document make up the legal basis of the EYFS (DfE, 2011b).

Providers must ensure that all practitioners understand the need to protect the privacy of the children in their care, as well the legal requirements that exist to ensure that information relating to the child is handled in a way that ensures confidentiality. Parents and/or carers must be given access to all records about their child, provided that no relevant exemptions apply to their disclosure under the DPA26 (DfE, 2012, p.26).

(See 'Confidentiality' in Chapter 2.)

Framework for observation and assessment

You will usually be observing activities that form part of the young child's everyday routine, making sure that the situations are realistic and not artificial. You can observe young children's development, learning and behaviour in a variety of situations.

For example, you might observe the following situations:

- A young child talking with another child or an adult.
- An adult working with a small group of young children.
- A child or a small group of children playing indoors or outdoors, or participating in a small or large group discussion, e.g. circle time.
- An adult reading or telling a story to a child or group of children.
- A child or group of children participating in a creative, literacy, mathematics or science activity, e.g. drawing, painting, early writing, number work or carrying out an experiment.

You should record your observations and assessments using an agreed format (see Chapter 4 for information on observation methods and techniques). Once you have recorded your observation of the child (or group of children), you need to make an assessment of this information in relation to:

- the aims of the observation, e.g. why you were doing this observation
- what you observed about the child's development, learning and/or behaviour in this particular activity
- how this compares to the expected level of development for a child of this age
- any factors that may have affected the child's ability to learn and/or behave, e.g. the immediate environment, significant events, illness, the child's cultural background, special needs.

The senior practitioner, setting manager or your college tutor/assessor will give you guidelines for the methods most appropriate to your role as an early years practitioner in your particular setting. Your observations and assessments must be in line with the setting's policy for record keeping and relevant to the routines and activities of the children you work with. You must follow the setting's policy regarding confidentiality at all times and be able to implement data protection procedures as appropriate to your role and responsibilities.

(Detailed information about confidentiality is given in Chapter 2.)

 Activity

Find out what your setting's policies are regarding child observations and assessments, confidentiality and record keeping and data protection procedures.

Gain information about developmental stage, progress, aspects of health/well-being and behaviour

Children's growth and development is **holistic**, with each area being interconnected. Remember to always look at the 'whole' child. You need to look at *all* areas of children's development in relation to the particular aspect of development or learning you are focusing on. For example, when observing a child's drawing or painting skills, as well as looking at their intellectual development you will need to consider the child's:

- physical development (fine motor skills when using a pencil or paintbrush)
- language development and communication skills (vocabulary and structure of language used to describe their drawing or painting, if appropriate)
- social and emotional development (interaction with others and behaviour during the drawing or painting activity).

(There is more detailed information about developmental stages in Chapter 5.)

 Key Term

Holistic: looking at the 'whole' child or young person, i.e. *all* aspects of the child's or young person's development – social and emotional, physical, intellectual, communication and language.

The importance of assessment

In the EYFS there are two types of assessment. The first is formative assessment, which practitioners should use on an ongoing basis to identify children's needs and to plan activities to meet them and to support children's future progress. The second is summative assessment, when practitioners take stock of children's overall progress at a particular point in time. The revised EYFS retains the requirement that practitioners undertake ongoing formative assessment, but aims to make clear that the paperwork should be kept to the absolute minimum required to promote children's successful learning and development (DfE, 2011b).

As well as being able to *observe* young children's development, you also need to *assess* children's development based on observational findings and other reliable information from children, parents, carers, colleagues and other appropriate adults. You must be able to make formative and summative assessments (see below) and record your assessments as appropriate to the policies and procedures of your setting. You should share your findings with the children and their parents as appropriate. You should also refer any concerns about children to senior colleagues and/or relevant external agencies when required. Always remember to follow the confidentiality and record keeping requirements of your setting.

Formative assessment

Formative assessments are initial and ongoing assessments. They identify future targets for the individual and groups as appropriate to the children's ages, developmental needs and abilities, *and* the requirements of the setting. Formative assessments are continuous and inform planning provision to promote children's development and learning. Examples of formative assessments include: child observations; tick charts/lists; reading records; mathematics records; daily target records for children with individual education plans.

Summative assessment

Summative assessments are assessments that summarise findings. They involve more formal monitoring of children's progress and are usually in the form of criterion-based tests or tasks. Examples of summative assessments include: the summary of development at age 24 to 36 months (see Chapter 7); the Early Years Foundation Stage Profile at the end of the EYFS (see Chapter 8); teacher assessments; annual school reports; reviews of children with special educational needs. (There is more information about assessing children's development in Chapter 6.)

Comparison with milestones, relation to child development theorists, achievement of curricular objectives, basis for planning future play/learning activities/provision

You will need to plan provision for the young children you work with based on your assessment of their developmental progress. You should recognise that young children's developmental progress depends on each child's individual level of maturation and their prior experiences. You should take these into account and have realistic expectations when planning activities and routines to promote young children's development. This includes regularly reviewing and updating plans for individual children and ensuring that plans balance the needs of each child and the group as appropriate to your setting.

You should know and understand that children develop at widely different rates but in broadly the same sequence. When planning provision to promote children's development you need to look at *all* areas of children's development (social, physical, intellectual, communication and language, and emotional development) in relation to the particular aspect of development or learning you are focusing on.

(There is more detailed information about the sequences of children's development, milestones of development and observing the different areas of learning in Chapter 5.)

 Activity

Find out more about the different areas of children's development, e.g. social development and behaviour; physical skills; intellectual abilities; communication skills and language development; emotional development. You could start by looking at Chapter 5 'Understand child and young person development' and Chapter 6 'Promote child and young person development' in *CACHE Level 3 Diploma: Children and Young People's Workforce – Early Learning and Child Care*; Chapter 1 'Extending understanding of theories of children and/or young person's care or development' in *CACHE Level 3 Extended Diploma: Children and Young People's Workforce – Early Learning and Child Care*.

Identifying developmental delay and significant learning or achievement

To participate fully in all aspects of education (and society) children need to successfully develop a wide range of abilities and skills. Adults working with children need to be aware of the factors that may affect children's growth and development. Depending on their individual experiences, and any special needs, some children may not have reached the same level of development as their peers. Some children may even be ahead of what is usually expected for children their age. Due to the wide range of experiences that children bring to the setting, it is important for you to have some knowledge and understanding of the possible reasons for these differences. Possible factors that may affect children's growth and development include: maturation; family and social circumstances; race and culture; the child care environment; and special needs.

You will probably observe a child or group of children on several occasions on different days of the week and at different times of the day. Use developmental charts for the child's age group (see Chapter 5) to identify areas of development where the child is making progress, as well as those where the child may be behind the norm for their age range. Remember to emphasise the positive; for example, a child with limited speech may still be developing positive social relationships with other children by using non-verbal communication during play activities.

Changes in behaviour

It is essential to observe and assess children not only to evaluate each child's learning needs but also to monitor their behaviour. As children develop, their needs and behaviour patterns change. Regular observations can help identify *pronounced* changes in a child's usual behaviour patterns.

Through accurate observation and assessment adults can:

- identify the child's main areas of difficulty
- respond to the child's behaviour in appropriate ways
- devise strategies to encourage the child to demonstrate more positive behaviour
- seek professional advice for a child with more persistent behavioural difficulties.

Basis of planning provision

Following your observation and assessment of a child's development, learning and/or behaviour, your recommendations can provide the basis for planning appropriate routines and/ or activities to encourage and extend the child's skills in specific areas. Effective planning in the foundation years is based on young children's individual needs, abilities and interests, hence the importance of accurate and reliable child observations and assessments. You will need to plan provision based on the relevant requirements for curriculum frameworks for early education, e.g. EYFS.

When planning care routines, play opportunities and learning activities, your overall aims should be to:

- support the care and development of *all* the children you work with
- ensure every child has full access to the appropriate curriculum
- meet children's individual developmental and learning needs
- build on each child's existing knowledge, understanding and skills.

 Activity

Describe how *you* plan provision to promote children's development in your setting. Include examples of any planning sheets you use.

How observation and assessment in early years settings should be underpinned by the four guiding themes of the EYFS

Observation and assessment in early years settings should be underpinned by the four guiding themes of the EYFS: a unique child; positive relationships; a positive environment; children develop and learn in different ways and at different rates.

The EYFS principles are designed to celebrate the importance of play and learning, by putting the young child at the heart of early years practice. With the publication of the *Curriculum Guidance for the Foundation Stage* in 2000, closely followed by *Birth to Three Matters* in 2003, a sound set of principles for effective early years provision was established, all of which celebrated the importance of play and active learning. The EYFS is a conscious attempt to set the principles that informed those guidelines in the foreground, by putting the child firmly back at the heart of practice (Jaeckle, 2008).

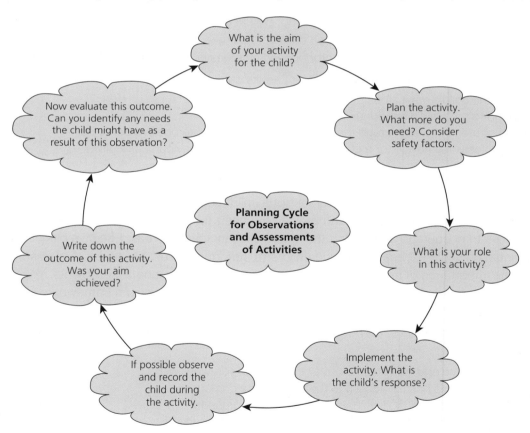

Figure 1.2 Planning children's activities (by J. Harding & L. Meldon-Smith)

Overarching principles

Four guiding themes shape the requirements of the EYFS, and should shape practice in early years settings (DfE, 2011b, p.4).

> Every child is a **unique child**, who begins learning at birth and can become resilient, capable, confident and self-assured.

Figure 1.3 Every child is a unique child

This principle celebrates the uniqueness of every child and advocates that practitioners take the time to observe, listen and tune in to individual children, in order to understand what it is that makes each child tick. As young children's strengths, interests, preferences and different developmental pathways begin to unfold, practitioners can plan responsively to capture experiences that are meaningful and tailored to individual needs. The EYFS encourages practitioners to constantly build on their previous best practice, through an ongoing process of reflection and self-evaluation, to improve the quality of their provision. This means that practitioners also need to be aware of their own unique strengths, capabilities and learning preferences (Jaeckle, 2008).

 Activity

Think about how observation and assessment in your setting is underpinned by the principle of 'a unique child', for example:

- How does the setting celebrate the uniqueness of every child?
- Do practitioners take the time to observe, listen to and tune in to individual children?
- How do practitioners identify the children's strengths, interests and preferences?
- How do practitioners plan for meaningful experiences that are tailored to the children's individual needs?
- What are *your* unique strengths, capabilities and learning preferences?

> Children learn to be strong and independent through **positive relationships** with their parents and carers and with others, including their key person at their early years setting.

Creating a secure emotional environment is paramount if everyone in the setting is to flourish. No one learns effectively when they are worried or afraid; both adults and children should be able to try new experiences, explore new resources and share their thoughts and feelings in an atmosphere of mutual trust and respect. When we are encouraged to think creatively and know that our ideas and contributions will be valued, we develop positive attitudes to learning and confidence in ourselves as learners. Mistakes are then seen in a positive light, as a natural part of the learning journey and an opportunity to grow and learn. A happy 'can do' attitude is infectious and everyone benefits – children, practitioners and parents (Jaeckle, 2008).

Figure 1.4 Children learn to be strong and independent through positive relationships with others

 Activity

Think about how observation and assessment in your setting is underpinned by the principle of 'positive relationships', for example:

● How does the setting create a secure emotional environment?
● Does the setting provide opportunities for both adults and children to try new experiences, explore new resources and share their thoughts and feelings?

A **positive environment** – in which children's experiences are planned to reflect their needs and help build their confidence, and in which there is a strong partnership between early years practitioners, parents and other professionals – is crucial if children are to fulfil their potential and learn and develop well.

In Reggio Emilia – the approach to early childhood education developed in the town of Reggio Emilia in northern Italy – the environment is sometimes referred to as the third teacher; and thoughtful planning, inside and out, is the key to really effective early years provision. The EYFS acknowledges the critical importance of both the emotional and the physical environment. Practitioners who view themselves as co-researchers working alongside the children will be able to see the environment from the child's point of view and reflect on the possibilities that it has to offer. When the environment is right, children are deeply engaged in their learning and practitioners' confidence soars as they are free to support each child constructively on their learning journey (Jaeckle, 2008).

 Activity

Think about how observation and assessment in your setting is underpinned by the principle of 'a positive environment', for example:

● Are there sufficient opportunities for children to get deeply involved, discover new lines of enquiry, experiment, explore and solve problems?
● Is the environment full of inspiration, with provocations for learning that will capture the child's imagination?
● Does the environment enable children to be independent and make their own choices of materials and resources?
● Are there quiet spaces where children can ponder and play as well as larger open spaces for them to test their new physical skills?

Figure 1.5 A positive environment is crucial if children are to fulfil their potential and learn and develop well

> **Children develop and learn in different ways and at different rates.** All areas of learning and development are important and are inter-connected.

Children learn from everything they do. The EYFS affirms that young children learn best through carefully planned, play-based experiences that start with their strengths, interests and capabilities. It acknowledges that young children are active learners and that they need opportunities to explore and make sense of the world, supported by knowledgeable, interested and sensitive adults. This principle recognises that all areas of learning are interconnected and that while children need to be taught new skills, these should always be balanced by opportunities for them to independently apply, practise and consolidate their new learning through a richly resourced environment, inside and out. The EYFS places the child firmly at the heart of the learning experience and demands an informed approach to supporting children's learning and development, gained through observational assessment and genuine partnerships with parents (Jaeckle, 2008).

 Activity

Think about how observation and assessment in your setting is underpinned by the principle of 'Children develop and learn in different ways and at different rates', for example:

- How do practitioners identify the children's different developmental pathways?
- How does the setting plan play-based experiences?
- How does the setting involve parents in the observation and assessment process?

Figure 1.6 Children develop and learn in different ways and at different rates

The assessment requirements of the EYFS

Assessment plays an important part in helping parents and practitioners to understand children's needs and to plan activities to meet these needs, thus supporting children's progress. The EYFS requires providers to assess children's progress on an ongoing basis, and also complete assessments at two specific points:

- When a child is aged between 24 and 36 months, practitioners must review progress in the prime areas, and supply parents or carers with a short written summary of their child's development.
- A report on progress is required is the final term of the year in which the child reaches age 5, and no later than 30 June in that term. At this point, the EYFS Profile must be completed for each child.

Observing children on an ongoing basis

The new EYFS framework makes clear that practitioners should observe and respond to each child in their care on an ongoing basis. It gives a broad steer that there should be a focus on prime areas for younger children, with gradual building in of support in the specific areas for older age ranges, as children develop, and as appropriate to their individual level of development and progress. This reflects the importance of the prime areas of learning for other areas, but practitioners should of course be flexible in their approach, responding to each child as an individual learner. There is nothing in the framework that holds a practitioner back from introducing specific areas to a particular child's learning experience earlier than they might for other children, if they judge that to be appropriate. Experiences that support younger children's learning in the prime areas, moreover, will also support their learning in the specific areas. Sharing rhymes and picture books, for example, lays the foundations for reading and writing as well as for communication and language (DfE, 2011b, Section 4).

Ongoing assessment (also known as formative assessment) is an integral part of the learning and development process. It involves practitioners observing children to understand their level of achievement, interests and learning styles, and to then shape learning experiences for each child reflecting those observations. In their interactions with children, practitioners should respond to their own day-to-day observations about children's progress and observations that parents and carers share. Assessment should not entail prolonged breaks from interaction with children, nor require excessive paperwork. Paperwork should be limited to that which is absolutely necessary to promote children's successful learning and development. Parents and/or carers should be kept up to date with their child's progress and development. Practitioners should address any learning and development needs in partnership with parents and/or carers, and any relevant professionals (DfE, 2012, p.10).

Summary of development at age 24 to 36 months

When a child is aged between 24 and 36 months, practitioners must review progress in the prime areas (personal, social and emotional development; physical development; communication and language) and supply parents or carers with a short written summary of their child's development. The purpose of the summary of development at age 24 to 36 months is to:

- identify any areas where the child's progress is less than expected
- plan to support that child's future learning and development in the setting
- help to ensure a good level of achievement by age 5 so that the child has a smooth transition to Key Stage 1.

The content of the summary of development must be based on the three prime areas of learning (and other areas as appropriate), reflecting the development level and needs of each individual child. The summary should highlight observations about a child's development, noting areas where a child is progressing well and where there are concerns about the child's development or learning. The summary should include a targeted plan to support that child's future learning and development in the setting.

Early identification of special educational needs (especially more complex needs) is very important as the earlier children receive tailored support to catch up, the stronger their subsequent chances of healthy development. As well as identifying any areas where practitioners are concerned that a child may have a developmental delay, special educational need, or disability, the summary includes activities and strategies the practitioner intends to adopt to address any issues or concerns.

Practitioners should discuss with parents how the summary of development can be used to support learning at home, as well as encouraging parents to share the summary of progress with other relevant professionals – including their health visitor and/or a teacher (if a child moves to school-based provision at age 3). With parental consent, practitioners can share information directly with health visitors, where possible, to help strengthen partnership-working between services, in order to support families.

(See Chapter 7 for detailed information about the summary of development at age 24 to 36 months.)

The assessment at the end of the EYFS

Assessment at the end of the EYFS, known as the Early Years Foundation Stage Profile, provides parents, practitioners and teachers with a well-rounded picture of a child's knowledge, understanding and abilities, their progress against expected levels, and their readiness for school. The Profile should help teachers to plan activities for children starting Key Stage 1. Providers must make arrangements for each child to be assessed throughout the final year (by a competent practitioner). The Profile report must reflect ongoing observation and should also take account of all relevant records held by the setting, and of any discussions with parents and other relevant adults.

Each child's level of development must be assessed (and recorded) against the 17 Early Learning Goals. Practitioners must indicate whether children are meeting expected levels of development, or if they are exceeding expected levels, or are not yet reaching expected levels ('expected', 'exceeding' or 'emerging').

Providers must supplement the Profile assessment with a short commentary on each child's skills and abilities in relation to the three key characteristics of effective learning, which are:

- **Playing and exploring** – children investigate and experience things, and 'have a go'.
- **Active learning** – children keep on trying if they encounter difficulties, and enjoy achievements.
- **Creating and thinking critically** – children have and develop their own ideas, make links between ideas, and develop strategies for doing things.

This commentary will give Year 1 teachers helpful background and context when considering each child's stage of development and learning needs.

The Profile must be completed for all children, including those with special educational needs and disabilities. Children will have differing levels of skills and abilities across the Profile and it is important that there is a full assessment of all areas of their development to inform plans for future activities. It is important that practitioners working with the child, and the child's parents, have a clear, rounded picture of all of a child's needs. Providers must share the Profile with parents, and explain to parents when and how they can discuss the Profile with the practitioner who completed it (DfE, 2011b).

(Detailed information about the Early Years Foundation Stage Profile is given in Chapter 8.)

Activity

Outline the assessment requirements in your setting.

CHAPTER 2

The principles of observing and assessing young children

This chapter will help you to understand the principles of observing and assessing young children, including:

* The principles of effective and purposeful child observation and assessment
* Planning for observation and assessment
* Undertaking observation
* Confidentiality.

Introduction

The principles of effective observation and assessment processes are interlinked with their purpose. Having a clear understanding of the purpose of observational assessment should be a guiding principle for all early years practitioners (Wall, 2006, p.93).

Observational assessment is integral to effective early years provision. Evidence clearly shows that observational assessment lies at the heart of providing a supporting and stimulating environment for every child and the objective of the Early Years Foundation Stage (EYFS) to create environments where practitioners understand children and can tailor their provision and teaching to support their development (Tickell, 2011, p.30).

Observation is the practice of looking at and listening to each child to find out:

1. How the child is developing.
2. What the child likes doing.
3. What the child is learning through play and the experiences on offer.

It is important that parents and practitioners share what they know about these three things so that they can decide whether the child's development is at the expected stage, whether the resources (such as toys and equipment) are suitable for the child and what to provide in the future to support the child to develop new interests, learn new skills and acquire new knowledge (EYM, 2012).

Assessment in the revised 2012 EYFS consists of two main types:

1. **Formative assessment** – ongoing assessment, which is what practitioners do on a daily basis to make decisions about what the child has learned or can do already so as to help the child move on in their learning; this type of assessment informs the next steps that are planned with the child and the parent.

2. **Summative assessment** – the summary of development at age 24 to 36 months (see Chapter 7) and the Early Years Foundation Stage Profile at the end of the EYFS (see Chapter 8); this type of assessment 'sums up' all the different information from ongoing assessments that have been made about the child.

(EYM, 2012)

The principles of effective and purposeful child observation and assessment

The principles for observing and assessing can be summarised as the need for practitioners to: be clear on the need for and purpose of assessing; ensure the appropriateness for the child; ensure the process is meaningful; consider ethical issues; ensure the validity of outcomes; use appropriate observational methods for the child and the setting; consider the timing of the observation as children can perform differently in mornings to afternoons, and on Mondays to Fridays; ensure there is adequate staffing to free the observer from additional responsibilities if necessary; and be clear on how the outcomes will be disseminated and to whom (Wall, 2006, p.94).

Seven principles for observation and assessment in the EYFS

1. Purposeful assessment.
2. Using ongoing observation to build up an accurate picture.
3. Using planned and spontaneous observations.
4. Making accurate judgements.
5. Taking equal account of all aspects of the children's development and learning.
6. Using contributions from a range of perspectives.
7. Involving children and their parents in the assessment process.

Purposeful assessment

Assessment must have a purpose. Assessment informs planning for the next steps in learning for each child, deepening and extending the child's learning. In practice this means:

- Practitioners listen to and note children's reactions to, and involvement in, their learning; they respond immediately in ways that support that learning.
- Assessment provides an insight into how best to help a child to develop and learn.
- The effectiveness of the setting's provision on children's development and learning is monitored carefully to ensure it has a positive impact.

(EYU, 2008)

Assessment needs to be recognised as a vital aspect of effective practice and provision throughout the EYFS:

- Assessment is not an end in itself nor an isolated activity for its own sake.
- Assessment is about observing and understanding the uniqueness of children at any age or stage and in any setting.
- Assessment is about a practitioner making sense of that understanding, acquired predominantly through observation, and using that information to support children's development.

- Assessment is a vital, vibrant and dynamic tool that enables practitioners to identify that uniqueness and ensure that provision supports, challenges and extends children's development and learning.

(Dubiel, 2008)

Some early years practitioners think they have to keep very detailed records of young children's activities to meet the requirements of the EYFS or to justify their judgements about children's level of development to others (for example, Ofsted and local authorities) or to illustrate to themselves and to parents how much progress children have made. According to Dame Clare Tickell, it is clear that if practitioners are spending considerable time writing things down then they should review their practice and ask

Figure 2.1 Purposeful assessment: listening to and noting children's reactions to their learning and responding immediately in ways that support that learning

whether the level of their record keeping is necessary. It is the interaction between practitioners and children that helps promote the rich learning environment the EYFS is seeking to create. This cannot be achieved if practitioners are making notes, instead of talking and playing with children (Tickell, 2011, p.30).

The revised 2012 EYFS states:

'Assessment plays an important part in helping parents, carers and practitioners to recognise children's progress, understand their needs, and to plan activities and support. Ongoing assessment… is an integral part of the learning and development process. It involves practitioners observing children to understand their level of achievement, interests and learning styles, and to then shape learning experiences for each child reflecting those observations.'

(DfE, 2012, p.10)

 A *Activity*

Discuss this question with colleagues: Does your assessment process have a clear purpose or is it just undertaken to satisfy Ofsted and/or other government requirements?

Using ongoing observation to build up an accurate picture

Ongoing observation of young children taking part in everyday activities is the most reliable way of building up an accurate picture of what children know, understand, feel, are interested in and can do over time and in a range of contexts. In practice this means:

- Practitioners make systematic observations and reflect on their interactions with children to understand each child's achievements, interests and learning styles.
- Observations and reflections capture the broad picture of children's development and learning, rather than narrow aspects.

- Observations are made in a range of contexts – when children are applying their knowledge, playing, eating together, going on outings, when they are engaged in experiences on their own and with others.

(EYU, 2008)

 Key Terms

Contexts: these are made up of people and provision. They create both the access to learning and the ethos in which the child learns.

Ethos: the characteristic spirit of a group of people or community, e.g. a happy ethos and/or a caring ethos.

Observing young children is the first step in the cycle of assessing their progress and needs and planning for their next steps before observing again. Child observations should be systematic, but a practitioner should not be sitting writing observations all day, or transcribing endless notes at home. As a practitioner you should make decisions about which children you will formally observe and when. For example, you might like to know more about a parent's comment about their child's interest in playing with water, and decide to observe the child playing with water and tubing alongside other children in the outdoor play area (Ragg, 2010, p.24).

The EYFS does not require children to be assessed against a grid or tick-list. Every child's learning journey is unique, and observation is used to identify the interests, learning patterns and schemas of the individual child. It can, however, be useful to regularly jot down information about individuals and groups in a brief form for later reference. An effective practitioner is prepared for the unexpected – sticky notes, pens and pencils, small observation forms (for focused snapshots) and longer ones (for detailed observations) should be to hand. A digital camera can help capture a moment, and a computer and printer are useful (Ragg, 2010, p.24).

(There is detailed information about observation methods in Chapter 4.)

 Key Term

Schemas: term used mainly by Piaget and Froebel to describe internal thought processes.

 Activity

Give examples of the methods your setting uses to facilitate ongoing observations to build up an accurate picture of each child's learning and development.

Using planned and spontaneous observations

Staff should both plan observations and be ready to capture the spontaneous but important moments. Everyday experiences and activities will provide an almost complete picture of the child's learning, but particular planning is needed to capture important aspects of learning that may not arise every day. In practice this means:

- Practitioners organise resources and their time so they can capture the planned and the spontaneous.
- Practitioners, especially the key persons, are deployed to carry out good quality observations.
- Practitioners realise that every interaction with children is an opportunity to learn about them and to influence the quality of their learning. Practitioners are trained to recognise important moments in children's development and learning.

(EYU, 2008)

Remember

As a practitioner, remember that you should not be observing children indiscriminately. You should stop and think:
- Why am I doing this observation?
- What does it tell me about this child's needs?
- How will it help me to plan for the child's next steps?
- How can I adapt my practice in light of this observation?

(Ragg, 2010, p.24)

 ## Activity

The child in Figure 2.2 is engrossed in an activity that involves the development of social skills. Think about:
- Do you need to plan further observations to assess the child's learning in this area?
- Which other activities might help encourage and extend the child's social skills?
- How would you plan for these activities?
- What resources would you need for these activities?
- Consider your role in implementing the selected activities.

Figure 2.2 Using planned and spontaneous observations

Making accurate judgements

Judgements of children's development and learning must be based on skills, knowledge, understanding and behaviour that are demonstrated consistently and independently. Assessments cannot be reliable or accurate if they are based on one-off instances or information gleaned solely from adult-directed activities. In practice this means:

- Practitioners make judgements about children's learning and plan for their next steps after considering a range of evidence displayed in different contexts.
- Children are observed in adult-directed activities and those they have initiated themselves.

(EYU, 2008)

Any judgements made by practitioners about young children's levels of development clearly need to be reliable in order to most effectively guide the children's continued progress as learners (Tickell, 2011, p.34). In order to do this, practitioners might use Development Matters in the Early Years Foundation Stage (see Further reading) throughout the EYFS as a guide to making best-fit judgements about whether a child is showing typical development for their age, or may be at risk of delay or is ahead for their age (Early Education, 2012, p.3).

Observations can help to clarify a child's current levels of performance and skills mastered. It should be remembered, however, that if interventions and provision are to be amended in the light of the observations, then practitioners should not assume that if a child has not mastered a particular skill that they are incapable of doing so. Before making a judgement about the child's learning and development, the practitioner should check that:

- The activity is child-appropriate (exactly at the right level to move the child forwards, i.e. stretching their knowledge and skills but without the risk of failure).
- The activity capitalises on the child's interests.
- The practitioners are supportive and encourage positive reinforcement.
- Any difficulties, such as a child's emotional development and/or self-concept, are not prohibiting the child from accessing the activity.
- The area/room encourages support and learning for that individual child.

(Wall, 2006, p.91)

For example, if a large group of young children is given the same worksheet to complete, then the child for whom the task is too difficult or too easy may become bored and restless. This may result in task-avoidance strategies or the manifestation of unacceptable behaviours. Two conclusions can be drawn from this scenario – the child has behaviour problems or the task is inappropriate for the child. Interpretation (or misinterpretation) of this simple example will clearly have significant effects on the child, practitioner and future planning. Therefore the skills of the observer, combined with their knowledge of the child and the setting, will be paramount (Wall, 2006, p.92).

 Activity

If you have not done so already, take a look at the sections in the Development Matters in the Early Years Foundation Stage (see Further reading) relevant to the children you mainly work with.

Taking equal account of all aspects of the children's development and learning

Effective assessment takes equal account of all aspects of the child's development and learning. A holistic approach to assessment is needed in order to reflect accurately the nature of children's development and to acknowledge the interrelationship between different aspects of learning. In practice this means:

- Practitioners tune in to the different skills children are developing – linguistic, interpersonal, creative, mathematical, scientific, critical thinking and technological.

- Practitioners do not set up assessments that dissect individual skills, but instead reflect on all the dimensions revealed by the normal activities in the setting.

(EYU, 2008)

Activity

- Reflect on the layout of your main activity room and discuss how observations of learning areas may help to develop an improved learning environment for the children in your setting.
- Identify one area of the activity room that you consider would benefit from change.

Using contributions from a range of perspectives

Accurate assessments are reliant on taking account of contributions from a range of perspectives. These assessments will include all adults who have contact with the child in a range of contexts, including the home, local authority and health professionals. In practice this means:

- Practitioners understand that all their interactions with children influence their development and learning.
- Practitioners respect the range of perspectives that adults in different roles will gain about children.
- Time is allocated so that practitioners can discuss what they know about individual children and consider the implications for the children's development and learning.

(EYU, 2008)

Observational assessments may also be shared with a range of supporting agencies working with the child and the family. For example, at progress review meetings or annual reviews for statements, evidence from all parties supporting children with special needs will be needed to inform further decision-making. Observational evidence will support this process with clear indicators of progress made, the child's likes and dislikes and strengths and weaknesses. When combined with reports from the child's parents and other professionals working with the child, the holistic picture can again emerge and inform decisions and planning (Wall, 2006, p.93).

Activity

Make a list of the types of contributions from a range of perspectives used in your setting, e.g. from children, parents, colleagues and other professionals.

Involving children and their parents in the assessment process

Children must be fully involved in their own assessment. Children should be involved in discussing their activities and how they feel about them from the beginning of their time in the setting. In practice this means:

- Practitioners and children are involved in conversations about learning; this helps children when they are involved in the activity, as well as when they review outcomes together.

- Adults model ways of working and discuss with children how they are exploring the learning.
- Children ask their own questions, talk about their thoughts and how they want to tackle a problem.
- Practitioners ask questions that encourage children to consider the quality and processes of their work and what to do next.

(EYU, 2008)

Dame Clare Tickell also supports the involvement of children in assessment activities, because it is both empowering for children and a good learning experience in itself (Tickell, p.31). You should consider the children's feelings; depending on the children's ages, needs and abilities, you should discuss the observation with the children to be observed and respond appropriately to their views, including these in your assessment.

Children should be aware that they are being observed, and should be encouraged to ask questions, make comments, and help to record their own learning journeys. For example, letting children stick photos into their own Profiles enables them to take ownership of their development, and makes them feel valued for their contribution. Remember to respect their preferences if they do not like having their photograph taken or if they want to take home that lovely painting that you were planning to include in their learning journey! (Ragg, 2010, p.24).

Assessments must actively engage parents in developing an accurate picture of the child's development. Effective partnership with parents will help to ensure that their vital perspective contributes to the overall description of their child's development and learning.

In practice this means:

- Practitioners engage in a two-way flow of information between family and setting, in order to meet children's needs effectively and agree the next steps in the child's learning.
- Practitioners talk to parents and involve them in reviews of their children's achievements, including those demonstrated at home.

(EYU, 2008)

A key person cannot observe absolutely everything – so observation needs to be a partnership between the practitioner and the child's parents or carers. They can offer alternative perspectives, or give further evidence to support your observations; for example, a colleague might observe a child doing something outdoors that builds on discussion that you have had with the child's parents (Ragg, 2010, p.24).

 Key Term

Key person: the member of staff with whom a child has more contact than other adults within the setting; this adult demonstrates a special interest in the child (and their family) through close daily interaction.

 Activity

- Are parents aware of ongoing observations and assessments that take place in your setting?
- If not, how could this situation be improved, to ensure all parents are included in the observation and assessment process?

Planning for observation and assessment

Observations of children are vital – as each child has a unique set of abilities and talents, observations in different situations will capture these first-hand. Observing what children choose to do, what their interests are, and with whom and with what resources they enjoy playing, provides adults with reliable information about children as individuals. The sections on 'Observing how a child is learning' in the Development Matters in the Early Years Foundation Stage document (see Further reading) can support developing systematic observations. Observation also provides opportunities to assess children's needs and so more accurately plan the next steps in their learning.

Observations should take place on a regular basis as part of daily routines. Discussing these with the child, their parents and colleagues gives a starting point for a holistic approach that will ensure that the child is always central to what is planned (EYM, 2012).

Ethical protocols

Before undertaking observations practitioners should ensure they have reflected on ethical issues, such as gaining permission from the child's parents and considering the responsibilities of the observer. Any parent has the right to refuse permission but this will be unlikely if the purposes and potential benefits of observations are explained thoroughly, as most parents will be supportive of initiatives that will encourage progress. The responsibilities of the observer include consideration of the safety of the children, confidentiality, appropriate behaviour and, perhaps most importantly, entering the process with an open mind. If practitioners have preconceived ideas or expectations of the outcomes then there is a risk that outcomes will be affected, or worse, invalid (Wall, 2006, p.94).

The early years setting should obtain permission from the parents/carers of the young children being observed, e.g. a letter requesting permission to do regular observations and assessments could be sent out for the parents to sign giving their consent. If you are an early years student, you must have the senior practitioner's and/or the parents' permission before making formal observations of children; before doing any portfolio activities for your course assessment involving observations of children you *must* negotiate with the senior practitioner or setting manager when it will be possible for you to carry out your observations and you must have written permission to do so.

 Activity

Prepare a letter that you can send to parents to formally request permission to complete regular observations and assessments of their child.

Where practitioners have to make decisions that are not clearly covered by statute on a case-by-case basis about sharing information, the decision to share or not share information must always be based on professional judgement. It should be taken in accordance with legal, ethical and professional obligations, supported by governmental information sharing guidance and informed by training and experience (DCSF, 2008a, p.28).

Activity

Take a look at the sections on 'Observing how a child is learning' relevant to the children you mainly work with in the Development Matters in the Early Years Foundation Stage (see Further reading).

Preparation of documentation, decision about aim, method and activity

Early years practitioners should: make systematic observations and assessments of each child's achievements, interests and learning styles; use these observations and assessments to identify learning priorities and plan relevant and motivating learning experiences for each child; and match their observations to the expectations of the Early Learning Goals (ELGs).

Where, when and how to make these observations and assessment will depend on the policies and procedures of the early years setting as well as your particular role within that setting, such as whether you work on your own as a childminder or as part of a team in a children's centre or working alongside a teacher in a Reception class. When working with others (for example, teachers, SENCO or relevant specialists) you will need to provide regular information about your work, such as updates about a particular child's progress. For example, when recording a child's behaviour

Figure 2.3 Thinking about observing (by J. Harding & L. Meldon-Smith)

using time or event sampling, you will need to agree specific dates and times on which observations will take place. Some information may be given orally, for example outlining a child's progress on a particular activity or commenting on a child's behaviour.

Activity

- What are the policies and procedures of your early years setting regarding observations and assessment? Outline the key points.
- What is your particular role in relation to observations and assessments? List your main responsibilities.

Importance of accurate and clear observations using accepted language and formats

You should record your observations and assessments using an agreed format. This might be a written descriptive account, structured profile (with specified headings for each section), or a pre-coded system of recording. Once you have recorded your observation of the child (or group of children), you need to make an assessment of this information in relation to:

- the aims of the observation, e.g. why you were doing this observation
- what you observed about the child's development, learning and/or behaviour in this particular activity
- how this compares to the expected level of development for a child of this age
- any factors that may have affected the child's ability to learn and/or behave, e.g. the immediate environment, significant events, illness, child's cultural background, special needs.

(There is more information about methods for observations and assessments in Chapter 4.)

Activity

List the methods for observations and assessments currently used in your setting.

Undertaking observation

Within the context of the EYFS, observation is about recording positively what you see and hear the child doing, not what the child cannot or does not do. An effective practitioner would observe: 'Ella counted to three today, using her fingers – wow!' not 'Ella can only count up to three' (Ragg, 2010, p.24).

Be positive when undertaking observation: focus on the children's strengths rather than just on any learning or behavioural difficulties they may have. Look at what children can do in terms of their development and/or learning and use this as the foundation for providing future activities.

You should also remember equal opportunities. Consider children's cultural backgrounds, for example children may be very competent at communicating in their community language, but may have more difficulty in expressing themselves in English; this does not mean they are behind in their language development. Consider how any special needs may affect children's development, learning and/or behaviour.

When writing up observations, reflect on your practice as well as describing what the child can do. Self-reflection will help you to think about what you are doing well and what you could do differently to improve children's experience and set goals for further achievement. Self-reflection will help improve your practice, provide evidence of the impact your work is having on children, and will also be very helpful in filling in the Ofsted self-evaluation form (Ragg, 2010, p.24).

Being unobtrusive, minimising distractions

When undertaking observations, you should minimise distractions. Observe children without intruding or causing unnecessary stress. Try to keep your distance where possible, but be close enough to hear the children's language. Try not to interact with the children (unless it is a participant observation – see Chapter 4), but if they do address you be polite and respond positively, e.g. explain to the children simply what you are doing and keep your answers short.

Observing activities that are part of the child's usual routine

Everyday experiences and activities will provide an almost complete picture of a child's learning, but particular planning is needed to capture important aspects of learning that may not arise every day. In a group setting, an adult-directed activity (such as asking the children to sort objects) can allow you to observe the children's skills in that particular area – which can then feed into assessment and tracking (Ragg, 2010, p.24).

(Information about adult-directed activity and child-initiated activity is given in Chapter 5.)

Objectivity/subjectivity

You should be objective – only record what you actually see or hear, not what you think or feel. For example, the statement 'The child cried' is objective, but to say 'The child is sad' is subjective, as you do not know what the child is feeling; children can cry for a variety of reasons, e.g. to draw attention to themselves or to show discomfort.

Accuracy, validity, reliability and purpose

Observations and assessments should have clear benefits for children's learning and development. Every observation and assessment should be tailored to a specific purpose and should be accurate, valid, reliable and fair to that purpose. Methods of observation and assessment should recognise that children need familiar contexts to be able to demonstrate their abilities (Morrison, 2007).

When observing and assessing young children's development, ensure that you include all aspects of development that you can remember, using the mnemonic SPICE:

- **S**ocial
- **P**hysical
- **I**ntellectual
- **C**ommunication and language
- **E**motional.

(See detailed information about observing different areas of learning in Chapter 5 and assessing children's progress in Chapter 6.)

Attitudes, values, beliefs and bias

Adults working with children, particularly in early education settings, have to make frequent judgements about children's achievements in comparison with other children. You must be *aware* of this social context, where the emphasis is on competition and 'good' academic results and *beware* of its effects on the expectations for children. Assessment, both formal and informal, creates labels for children that can affect adult expectations; such labelling may affect children adversely for years to come.

You can avoid bias and encourage positive attitudes, values and beliefs by:

- Respecting all children as valued and important individuals.
- Promoting children's care, learning and development in appropriate ways.
- Creating awareness of the effects of adult expectations, e.g. adults need to be aware of bias within the childcare setting (and society as a whole) and to avoid stereotypical assumptions.
- Working within the cultural and social context of the setting, e.g. *use* the children's backgrounds positively; know that limitations exist, but *use* them to advantage even with the constraints of the EYFS.
- Actively promoting equal opportunities.
- Using the children's own perceptions of themselves, e.g. acknowledging their personal views of their individual capabilities.
- Using friendship or temperament groups instead of ability groups.
- Giving children more choice over their activities and involving them in decision-making.

 Key Term

Social context: any situation or environment where social interaction occurs, e.g. home, early years setting, local community.

 Activity

Give examples of how your setting avoids bias and encourages positive attitudes, values and beliefs.

Confidentiality

Confidentiality must be maintained at all times. Records must be easily accessible and available (with prior agreement from Ofsted, these may be kept securely off the premises). Confidential information and records about staff and children must be held securely, and only be accessible and available to those who have a right or professional need to see them. Providers must be aware of their responsibilities under the Data Protection Act (DPA) 1998 and, where relevant, the Freedom of Information Act 2000 (DfE, 2012, p.26).

Security of information

You need to know the exact policy and procedures for storing records in the setting. You should also know what your own role and responsibilities are regarding the storage of records. You must maintain the safe and secure storage of observations and assessments at all times. You should not leave important documents lying around; always put them back in storage after use. As well as the physical security of records, you need to be aware of the levels of staff access to information. You should never give out the passwords to the setting's equipment (e.g. computers) unless you have permission from the member of staff responsible for the record keeping systems.

(More detailed information about record keeping is in Chapter 3.)

Disclosure of information

Spoken information needs to be given in a professional manner, that is: to the appropriate person (senior colleague or SENCO); in the right place (not in a corridor where confidential information could be overheard); and at the right time (urgent matters need to be discussed with the appropriate person as soon as possible, while others may wait until a team meeting).

Requests for records or reports should be dealt with professionally and handed in on time. This is particularly important if the information is needed for a meeting or review as any delay may stop others from performing their responsibilities effectively. Always remember to maintain confidentiality as appropriate to the setting's requirements.

Confidential record keeping and storage is important: only the appropriate people should have access to confidential records. Except where a child is potentially at risk, information should not be given to other agencies unless previously agreed. Where the passing of confidential information is acceptable then it should be given in the agreed format. Always follow the setting's policy and procedures regarding confidentiality and the sharing of information; check with your line manager if you have any concerns about these matters.

(See more detailed information about reporting concerns in Chapter 3.)

 Activity

What is your setting's policy for the storage and security of child records?

Record keeping and information sharing

This chapter will help you to understand the importance of record keeping and information sharing, including:

* The principles of record keeping
* The importance of record keeping
* Confidentiality and permissions for record keeping
* Sharing information as appropriate to the policies and procedures of the setting
* Legislation relating to the use of personal information
* Reporting concerns.

Introduction

Record keeping is an essential part of observation and assessment in the early years setting. Records ensure that an accurate and up-to-date profile of individual children's learning is available, which provides the basis for the reporting of children's learning and development to parents and carers. Records help early years practitioners to monitor children's progress and to intervene or seek expert help when necessary (Smidt, 2005).

Early years settings keep many types of records relating to young children, including essential information such as emergency contact details, addresses, parental consent for outings, and information on health and other issues. Settings must also keep records relating to each child's learning and development; these records are compiled from the observations and assessments (as described in the previous chapters) and should be collected over time. Record keeping refers to the processes and systems that the setting or individual practitioner puts in place for compiling these records of learning and development. It is much better if one system (however multi-faceted) has been agreed and is implemented by all staff concerned. If your record keeping processes and systems are to work for you, rather than you working for them, they have to be manageable and useful for planning (Hutchin, 1999).

The principles of record keeping

Working with young children involves several aspects of record keeping, including regularly observing children and taking notice of what they say and do. You will have a system in place whereby you write down your observations and use these as the basis for deciding what each child you have observed needs to do next, and you should also be involved in building up profiles of children's work. A profile is a collection of things related to an individual child, which taken together give a detailed account of the child's progress and development. These include activities done by

Tom's One-Page Profile

Photo

What people like and admire about me...
Polite, caring, good at remembering things
Good at playing games
Good at drawing and building stuff
Creative, thoughtful, careful

What is important to me...
Having two kittens called Tak and Zim
Playing video games and board games with my Mum or Dad
Watching TV, especially *Digimon*
Playing with my best friend, Jamie
Having Sunday lunch at my Nan's house
Going to Colchester every year to visit my Granny, Aunty Rebecca and Uncle Jonathan
My computer and using Paint at home several times a week
My toys, especially Digimon figures and Lego
Knowing what is going to happen each day, and planning ahead for special things like my birthday and days out

How to support me well...
I am very sensitive and a small negative comment seems like a big telling-off
I needs lots of praise and encouragement
I do not like change very much and need lots of reassurance about changing classes
I am quiet and shy before you get to know me, and I need you to initiate conversations
I like talking about things that interest me, especially video games and Digimon

Figure 3.2 Example of a child's one-page profile (adapted from Sanderson, Smith & Wilson, 2010, pp.9 and 30)

Top tips

What are your top tips and ideas about how to support your child at nursery?

Figure 3.3 Form involving parents in gathering information (adapted from Sanderson, Smith & Wilson, 2010, p.22)

Activity

As a group explore various ways to involve parents in record keeping, for example:
- Sending the form home.
- Inviting parents in in groups.
- Making individual appointments.
- Considering the requirements of working parents, single parents, parents who prefer not to come out when it is dark, etc.
- Providing a crèche.
- Providing translators and interpreters.

Since the Children Act children have had a right to be heard, but perhaps there is an assumption that very young children are not mature enough, nor knowledgeable or verbally capable of contributing anything of value to observations and assessments. It must also be acknowledged that there are discrete differences between listening to and truly hearing and understanding what a child is saying (Wall, 2006, p.106).

Involving children in profiling is a complex task and requires considerable thought and planning. Where it is done well, children say interesting and revealing things and their comments or pieces of work add enormously to the sense of that child's achievement over a period of time (Smidt, 2005, p.86).

You can gather information about the child by:
- Using activities from 'It's Great to Be Me' as part of the SEAL curriculum.
- Having one-to-one conversations using fill-in sheets to record information or using posters that children can complete about themselves. Parents/carers and volunteers may be able to help with this (see Figure 3.4).
- Using 'appreciation stickers'. These stickers were developed for and by Norris Bank School and are a way for teachers to write the specific characteristic or behaviour that they are rewarding. These are saved on to a card and can inform the 'what people like and admire about me' section of the one-page profile.

(Sanderson, Smith & Wilson, 2010, p.6)

For very young children (especially those with special needs) difficulties may occur due to limited verbal skills and recording skills, but ways can be developed by which such children can be empowered and feel a part of the process. Knowing a child's likes and dislikes can enable more successful progress through heightened motivation for the child to participate. So it would be of greater use to plan activities that the child would prefer, in order for them to achieve targets, than it would be to continually present them with tasks they do not particularly enjoy. For very young children, likes and dislikes can be discovered through simple pictorial records, which can be added to the child's records and shared with parents and other practitioners. Simple drawings or photographs of a range of common activities can be presented alongside three faces – one happy, one indifferent and one sad.

The activity can be discussed with the child and then he/she could colour in the appropriate face to indicate his/her preferences. To ensure understanding, an adult could complete a similar chart alongside the child, making sure that the child is not simply copying the adult's selections.

All about me,
my family and friends

my name ....

my age

....

my birthday

....

what my family love about me

....
....
....
....

my best friends...

if I was an animal I would be (draw it here)

my favourite things...

yummiest food

good places to go

best teacher

things to take on holiday

when I grow up...

1

2

3

my 3 wishes are...

my best kept secret (shhhh)

things that make me laugh...

Figure 3.4 Form involving children in gathering information (from Sanderson, Smith & Wilson, 2010, p.33)

Young children can also be involved in progress recording through progress books, collecting and presenting evidence of their work in portfolios, responding to interviews (to identify their likes, dislikes and views) and through the self-completion of charts. Circle time can be a valuable tool to facilitate listening to others and even children with limited or no communication skills and withdrawn children can still participate, albeit in a different way. If appropriate, the practitioner can tell the group what the child has achieved and how much effort they have made. This way all children can be positively rewarded through the respect of being heard and their efforts being acknowledged and valued (Wall, 2006, pp.106–7).

Figure 3.5 Acknowledging and valuing children's efforts and achievements

 *Activity*

Give examples of how your setting involves young children in the record keeping process.

The importance of record keeping

Record keeping systems and procedures are essential to:

- monitor each child's learning and developmental progress
- provide accurate, detailed information regarding children's learning and behaviour
- determine the effectiveness of an activity or target
- determine the effectiveness of adult support or intervention

- give constructive feedback to the child
- share information with other practitioners, other professionals and parents
- identify and plan for new learning objectives or behaviour targets.

Tool to help practitioners, children and their parents to reflect on children's attainment and progress

The record keeping process should provide opportunities for children to share and review their own learning as well as identify their own emerging learning needs. Observations can be shared with parents to discuss progress made and to consider parental observations from outside the setting. A child may demonstrate skills at home, but not in the setting, for a variety of reasons, such as self-confidence. This information will help the practitioner to create a holistic picture of the child. In addition, parents and practitioners can work together to maximise progress. It may be that a child is reluctant to participate in dressing up due to issues of gender and/or culture, so the practitioner should seek information from discussions with parents. Information gained will then enable greater understanding on the part of the practitioner and setting, combined with an acknowledgement and respect of these important family factors. For example, a child whose grandfather is seriously ill in hospital may be distressed by stories about doctors and/or role play. With practitioner understanding these needs can easily be supported (Wall, 2006, p.92).

Confidentiality and permissions for record keeping

As a practitioner, you will be involved in maintaining record keeping systems, including helping with the range of written records used within the early years setting to monitor individual children, learning activities, resources and requisitions.

Early years settings also have records relating to the assessment of children's learning and development within the EYFS framework (see formative and summative assessments in Chapter 1). The record keeping systems and procedures you need to follow will depend on the exact planning and assessment requirements of the setting, senior practitioners, teachers, SENCOs and any other professionals involved in meeting the children's learning and development needs. It is important to update records on a regular basis; the frequency of updating depends on the different types of records that you make a contribution towards. Records that may indicate potential problems with individual children should be shown to a senior practitioner or the class teacher (e.g. observations of unacceptable behaviour; daily records that show poor performance).

 Activity

- Find out about the record keeping systems and procedures used within your setting.
- Give examples of the types of records used for the children with whom you work.

Confidentiality

Confidential information is information that is not normally in the public domain nor readily available from any other source, it may have a degree of sensitivity and value and be subject to a duty of confidence. A duty of confidence arises when one person provides information to another in circumstances where it is reasonable to expect that the information will be held in confidence (DCSF, 2008a, p.32).

Good communications are essential in any learning community, but some information needs to be shared widely while other information must have a restricted audience. Practitioners working with young children will often come into contact with confidential information. The early years setting should strive to protect everyone's right to privacy and not to have information about them or the setting lightly passed on to others. The principles of confidentiality and privacy are paramount and should be second nature to all staff working in the setting.

The setting's prime objective is to ensure the welfare and well-being of individual children, their families and the setting as a whole. Information about a child, or a member of their family, should be shared only on a 'need to know' basis. Equally, information relating to the setting should be treated as confidential where the passing on of that information risks damaging the setting or any of its members. If in doubt, the question should be asked in all cases: 'Is it in the child's best interest to pass on this piece of information?' If not, than the general presumption is to keep the information to oneself.

Permissions

The setting should have a clear Confidentiality Policy that is known and understood by all members of the setting. To ensure that all matters relating to confidentiality are subject to the setting's main commitment to the safety and well-being of each child, everyone should also be aware of the setting's Safeguarding Children or Child Protection Policy. Knowledge and understanding of these policies will ensure that all those using and working in the setting can do so with confidence. This means that all staff must respect confidentiality in the following ways:

- Parents only have access to the files and records of their own children as outlined in the setting's Record Keeping Policy.
- Practitioners will not discuss individual children with people other than the parents/guardians of that child.
- Information given by parents to the staff will be treated with sensitivity and will not be passed on to other adults without permission.
- Any anxieties about or evidence relating to a child's personal safety will be kept in a confidential file and will not be shared within the setting except by the child's key person and the setting's manager.
- Students on placement at the setting, parent helpers and other volunteers will be advised of the Confidentiality Policy and required to respect and maintain it. Breaches of confidentiality or lack of respect for privacy will lead to the student's, parent's or volunteer's services being discontinued.
- Issues to do with employment of staff, whether paid or unpaid, will remain confidential to the people directly involved in making personnel decisions.

Partnership with parents

Early years providers must maintain records and obtain and share information (with parents and carers, other professionals working with the child, and the police, social services and Ofsted as appropriate) to ensure the safe and effective management of the setting, and to help ensure that the needs of all children are met. Providers must enable a regular two-way flow of information

Record Keeping Policy
Person Responsible: Headteacher
Introduction
The school will keep the following records:
- Pupil Admission Documents
- Pupil Education Records
- Curriculum Policy Documents
- Non-curricular Policy Documents
- Personnel Records
- Financial Records.

Pupil Admission Documents
The school will keep admission records that specify any personal information required by the DfE, local authority or school governors relating to pupils on roll at the time. These records will be kept up-to-date and amended as and when pupils join or leave the school, providing the keeping of such information does not contravene any law applicable at the time.

Pupil Education Records
The school will keep and update educational records on pupils, covering their abilities, progress, academic achievements and other skills in school. These records may include:
- Pupil profiles
- Formative records
- Summative records
- Examples of work
- Copies of school reports
- Record of achievement.

The school will provide an opportunity for the correction of inaccurate educational and personal records. The school governors shall consider appeals against any decision by the headteacher or any teacher with delegated authority to refuse to disclose, transfer, copy or amend a pupil's record.

Curriculum Policy Documents
The documents that describe the school's policies on curriculum subject areas, topics, schemes of work, etc., will be kept up-to-date and are available for inspection by authorised persons (e.g. parents, advisors, inspectors and governors). The headteacher keeps a master copy of each document in his/her office and these are available for inspection by authorised and appropriate personnel upon request.

Non-curricular Policy Documents
The documents that describe the school's policies on non-curricular matters as required by the governing body, local authority, Ofsted or DfE will be prepared, maintained and kept up-to-date and made available to authorised persons as required. A list of the required policies is also available and is updated as appropriate.

Personnel Records
The school will maintain records of personnel, relating to their qualifications, experience, length of service, salary levels. References for staff within the school for posts outside it will be kept securely by the headteacher and will not be kept with the personnel records.

Appraisal statements are the property of the appraisee and will not be stored with the above records and cannot be used in any way other than at the request of, or with the permission of, the appraisee. A single copy of appraisal statements may be kept securely in the school office. Records of appraisal statements must not be kept on computer disc or system.

Application forms of applicants (including references) for vacant posts will be kept securely in the school office until an appointment has been made. Following a successful interview the successful candidate's application and references will be forwarded to the local authority personnel department and the others kept for no less than 6 months securely within the school with access by the headteacher only. Any copies of these applications will be destroyed following a successful appointment.

Financial Records
The records of the school's financial controls and budget will be kept in accordance with current DfE and local authority regulations and will be made available for inspection by the proper authorities under those statutes and regulations.

Confidentiality
Confidential reports (e.g. from Social Services, psychological reports, etc.) must be kept separately from the above general pupil information. Sensitive information, such as details of pupils with special educational needs, will be handled carefully.

A pupil's educational records (except for exempted material as specified in law) will be disclosed on request to their parents within the time specified by the statute in force at the time, and to schools considering a pupil for admission or following a request from another school after transfer.

Under the Data Protection Act 1998 certain information is exempt from disclosure and should not be shared with other service providers. This includes:

- Material whose disclosure would be likely to cause serious harm to the physical or mental health or emotional condition of the pupil or someone else.
- Information about whether the child is or has been subjected to or may be at risk of suspected child abuse (see Child Protection Policy).
- References about pupils supplied to another school, any other place of education or training, any national body concerned with student admissions.
- Information that may form part of a court report.

Further information on confidentiality issues is available in the school's Confidentiality Policy.

Figure 3.6 Example of Record Keeping Policy

with parents and/or carers, and between providers, if a child is attending more than one setting. If requested, providers should incorporate parents' and/or carers' comments into children's records (DfE, 2012, p.26).

Providers must make the following information available to parents and/or carers:

- How the EYFS is being delivered in the setting, and how parents and/or carers can access more information (for example, via the DfE website).
- The range and type of activities and experiences provided for children, the daily routines of the setting, and how parents and carers can share learning at home.
- How the setting supports children with special educational needs and disabilities.
- Food and drinks provided for children.
- Details of the provider's policies and procedures including the procedure to be followed in the event of a parent and/or carer failing to collect a child at the appointed time, or in the event of a child going missing at, or away from, the setting.
- Staffing in the setting; the name of their child's key person and their role; and a telephone number for parents and/or carers to contact in an emergency.

(DfE, 2012, p.27)

It is essential for all members of staff (including agency or supply staff) to be aware of some information about individual children, to help them achieve their potential and to take care of their social, emotional and health needs. Essential information includes medical conditions requiring special measures, e.g. diabetes, epilepsy, asthma, severe allergic reactions (anaphylaxis), and where emergency medication is kept in the setting; sensitive family situations, e.g. bereavement, severe illness, parents separating or divorcing; and custody problems, e.g. parents who are by law not allowed access to their children.

Early years providers must record the following information for each child in their care: full name; date of birth; name and address of every parent and/or carer who is known to the provider (and information about any other person who has parental responsibility for the child); which parent(s) and/or carer(s) the child normally lives with; and emergency contact details for parents and/or carers (DfE, 2012, p.27).

Parents may look through their child's records and may request photocopies of all or part of the file subject to any legal requirements as outlined in the setting's Record Keeping Policy. Parents may look through their own child's work at any time that is mutually convenient for them and the key person, usually at the designated open evenings and parents' evenings. Apart from work that is on

GREEN LEAS PLAYGROUP
REGISTRATION FORM

PERSONAL DETAILS
Child's Name: _____
Home Address: _____
_____
Home Telephone: _____ Date of Birth:_____

CONTACT DETAILS
1. Parent/Guardian's Name:

   Address: _____
   Home Telephone: _____ Work Telephone: _____
2. Parent/Guardian's Name:

   Address: _____

EMERGENCY CONTACT DETAILS
1. Name: _____
   Home/Work Tel.: _____ Mobile Tel.: _____
2. Name: _____
   Home/Work Tel.: _____ Mobile Tel.: _____
3. Name: _____
   Home/Work Tel.: _____ Mobile Tel.: _____

MEDICAL DETAILS
GP's Name: _____
Address: _____
GP Telephone: _____
Please state any known medical conditions or allergies: _____
_____
Please state any special dietary requirements, including the child's food
preferences: _____
_____
I give my consent to any emergency treatment required for my child
_____ *while at the Green Leas Playgroup.* Yes/No
Signed_____ Dated _____

**All records are confidential and kept in accordance with the Data Protection
Act 1998.**

Figure 3.7 Example of a registration form

display, the work of individual children is not available for other parents to read or look through. In no circumstances is it acceptable for parents to look through another child's tray without the specific agreement of that child's parents.

 Activity

- Outline your setting's policy and procedures for reporting children's progress to their parents.
- What are your responsibilities for reporting children's progress to their parents?

Sharing information as appropriate to the policies and procedures of the setting

You may be working as part of a team with other professionals including other early years practitioners, teaching assistants, teachers and SENCOs. Your colleagues will need regular information about your work, e.g. feedback about play activities as well as updates about child participation and/or developmental progress. Some of this information may be given orally, for example outlining a child's participation and developmental progress during a particular activity or commenting on a child's behaviour. Even spoken information needs to be given in a professional manner, to the appropriate person, in the right place and at the right time. Some information will be in written form, e.g. activity plans, notice boards, newsletters, staff bulletins and records.

There should be very close teamwork in the setting and all practitioners should know all the children. You should continually liaise with other members of staff and use your assessment information to inform planning for the children concerned. All records should be passed on to the relevant member of staff, e.g. the child's Reception teacher. Working with senior colleagues, you will need to ensure that full and complete records are provided for the new setting when children transfer to another nursery or primary school. You may need to share information about children's progress with other professionals, e.g. when working with children with special educational needs or when reporting concerns about a child's welfare. You must follow your setting's policies and procedures for sharing information, including any confidentiality and data protection requirements (see below).

Sharing information is an important part of early intervention and preventative services. There is an increasing emphasis on integrated working across services, with the aim of delivering more effective intervention at an earlier stage. Early intervention aims to prevent problems escalating and to increase the chances of achieving positive outcomes. In some areas there is increased use of multi-agency services, for example in children's centres to support children's health and development (DCSF, 2008a, p.6).

Parents usually know more about their children and their children's needs so it is important to listen to what parents have to say. You should therefore actively encourage positive working relationships between parents (or designated carers) and the setting. Remember to pass on information from parents to the relevant member of staff. Always remember **confidentiality** with regard to information provided by parents or carers.

Only give information to a parent that is consistent with your role and responsibilities within the setting – do not give recommendations concerning the child's future learning needs directly to the parents if this is the responsibility of the teacher, a senior colleague or other professional. Any information shared with parents must be agreed with the senior practitioner/setting manager and must comply with the confidentiality requirements of the setting. When sharing information about a child with his or her parents ensure that it is relevant, accurate and up-to-date.

Figure 3.8 Sharing information with parents

Policies and procedures of the setting

Practitioners need to understand their organisation's position and commitment to information sharing. They need to have confidence in the continued support of their organisation where they have used their professional judgement and shared information professionally (DCSF, 2008a, p.25).

To give practitioners confidence to apply the guidance in practice, it is important that their employers aim to establish:

- A culture that supports information sharing between and within organisations, including proactive mechanisms for identifying and resolving potential issues and opportunities for reflective practice.
- A systematic approach within their agency to explain, when the service is first accessed, to service users how and why information may be shared, and the standards that will be adopted, which will help to build the confidence of all involved.
- Clear systems, standards and procedures for ensuring the security of information and for sharing information. These may derive from the organisation's information sharing governance, any local procedures in place, or from their professional code of conduct.
- Infrastructure and systems to support secure information sharing, for example, access to secure email or online information systems.
- Effective supervision and support in developing practitioners' and managers' professional judgement in making these decisions. For example, access to training where practitioners can

discuss issues that concern them and explore case examples with other practitioners; and specific training and support for managers and advisors who provide support to practitioners in making information sharing decisions.

● Mechanisms for monitoring and auditing information sharing practice.
● A designated source of impartial advice and support on information sharing issues, and for resolution of any conflicts about information sharing.

(DCSF, 2008a, p.25)

 Key Term

Information sharing protocol: a signed agreement between two or more organisations or bodies, in relation to specified information sharing activity and/or arrangements for the routine of bulk sharing of personal information.

Legislation relating to the use of personal information

Providers must ensure that practitioners understand the need to protect the privacy of the children in their care as well the legal requirements that exist to ensure that information relating to the child is handled in a way that ensures confidentiality. Parents and/or carers must be given access to all records about their child, provided that no relevant exemptions apply to their disclosure under the Data Protection Act 1998. Records must be easily accessible and available (with prior agreement from Ofsted, these may be kept securely off the premises). Confidential information and records about staff and children must be held securely, and be only accessible and available to those who have a right or professional need to see them. Providers must be aware of their responsibilities under the Data Protection Act (DPA) 1998 and, where relevant, the Freedom of Information Act 2000 (DfE, 2012, p.26).

If you are asked, or wish, to share information about a person, you need to have a good reason or a clear and legitimate purpose to do so. This will be relevant to whether the sharing is lawful in a number of ways. If you work for a statutory service, for example education, social care, health or justice, the sharing of information must be within the functions or powers of that statutory body that is sharing the information as a normal part of your job. This will also be the case if you work in the private or voluntary sector and are contracted by one of the statutory agencies to provide services on their behalf. Whether you work for a statutory or non-statutory service, any sharing of information must comply with the law relating to confidentiality, data protection and human rights (DCSF, 2008a, p.14).

(There is more information about the legal framework for sharing information in the document *Information Sharing: Further Guidance on Legal Issues* – see Further reading.)

There are some circumstances where access to educational records may be restricted:

> *'The Secretary of State may by order exempt from the subject information provisions, or modify those provisions in relation to personal data in respect of which the data controller is the proprietor of, or a teacher at, a school, and which consist of information relating to persons who are or have been pupils at the school...'*

(Section 30(2) Data Protection Act, 1998)

by the child during the observation with the levels of expected development (e.g. how this child's abilities compare to the drawing or painting skills and intellectual development expected for children of this particular age).

4. **The 'verdict'.** From this comparison, draw your own conclusions regarding this child's development, learning and/or behaviour; state whether you think the child's abilities are ahead, equal to or behind the expected level of development as outlined by the experts. Remember to be tactful in your comments and also to be positive! Your conclusions should focus on what the child *can* do. Do not forget to mention other factors that might have affected the child's development, learning and/or behaviour in general or in this particular activity. Comment on how other aspects of the child's development affected the child's abilities in the focus area (e.g. poor concentration or limited motor skills).

Figure 4.1 Observations involve gathering and analysing evidence

Your assessment may include charts, diagrams and other representations of the data you collected from your observation (see examples of observation charts below). Your college tutor or assessor should give you guidelines on how to present your observations. Otherwise you might find the suggested format in Table 4.1 useful.

Observational methods

Child observations are an important way to increase both holistic knowledge and understanding of young children in order to assess a variety of areas including communication skills, cognitive skills, emotional development and social development. Observations and assessments also help to identify children with special needs and how children's behaviour changes in group settings. There are several different approaches to child observation, including using narrative reports, time sampling, checklists, event sampling and verbatim reporting (Le Page, 2010b).

 Activity

List the observation methods used in your setting.

Written narrative

For most practitioners observation is a feature of everyday working life and practitioners can often be found with a notebook and pen close to

Figure 4.2 Student observing a young child

hand to jot down unplanned observations that can be added to normal recording systems at a later time. As previously discussed, however, specific observations should be planned. Before starting an observation, the practitioner should select the most appropriate observational method from the range available (Wall, 2006, p.95).

Number/title of observation:
Date of observation:
Method: e.g. written narrative, running record, diary, target child, time sample, event sample, checklist, longitudinal, mapping, field notes.
Start time:
Finish time:
Number of children/adults:
Permission for observation: e.g. parent, senior practitioner and/or teacher.
Type of setting and age range: e.g. pre-school playgroup, day nursery, children's centre, Reception class in primary school.
Immediate context/background information: including the activity and its location.
Description of child/children: including first name(s) or initials, age(s) in years and months.
Aims: why are you doing this particular observation?
Observation: the actual observation, e.g. written, chart, graph or audio/video recording.
Assessment: include the following: ● Did you achieve your aims? ● Comparison of the child's development with the expected development of a child of this age, looking at all aspects of the child's development but with particular emphasis on the focus area (e.g. physical, social and emotional or communication and intellectual skills). ● References to support your comments.
Personal learning: what you gained from doing this observation, e.g. what you have learned about this aspect of development and using this particular method of observing children, e.g. was this the most appropriate method of observation for this type of activity?
Recommendations: ● On how to encourage/extend the child's development, learning and/or behaviour in the focus area, e.g. suggestions for activities to develop the child's communication skills. ● For any aspect of the child's development, learning and/or behaviour that you think requires further observation and assessment.
References/bibliography: list details of all the books used to complete your assessment.

Table 4.1 Suggested format for recording observations

The narrative method is often referred to as 'free description'. It is likely to be one of the first methods you try. It allows you to record events or structured activities as they happen. It is written in the present tense, and so provides a lively account of what is happening. You must remember to be objective in your recording and only write what you see and hear (Harding & Meldon-Smith, 2001, p.55).

Title of observation: Observing a young child's communication skills while playing	
Date of observation: 10 October 2012	
Method: written narrative	
Start time: 10:40 a.m.	
Finish time: 10:45 a.m.	
Number of children/adults: 3 children and 1 adult	
Permission for observation: nursery teacher	
Type of setting and age range: nursery class in primary school	
Immediate context/background information: sand tray in 'messy' area of the nursery	
Description of child: Tom, aged 4 years and 3 months	
Aims: To observe a young child's communication skills while playing with other children	

Observation:

Tom walks slowly across to the sand tray, looking around him as he moves forwards. He looks at Alex, smiles and stops in front of him. Tom touches Alex's arm with his left hand and speaks quietly into his right ear:

'Come on Alex, will you play in the sand? We can make big, deep holes for dinosaurs!'

Alex pushes him away forcefully and Tom stumbles backwards and grabs hold of the side of a table. Tom's mouth turns downwards and his eyes water slightly. He gulps several times, then shouts loudly:

'I'll never be your friend ever now!'

Tom looks across at Ms K. and starts to move towards her. He turns to face the sand tray again, looks around him and stares at Jamie. He calls clearly across to Jamie:

'Hey, Jamie! Please do you want to see the huge dinosaur buried in the sand? He's hiding from the people in Jurassic Park.'

Jamie comes across to him. He takes his hand, smiling broadly and they skip together towards the sand tray.

(Continued)

Assessment:

I observed that Tom's communication and social interaction (plus other aspects of development) were in line with the expected development for a child aged 4 to 5 years.

Communication and language development:

Tom showed good communication skills when he approached Alex and Jamie. He used body language to signal that he wanted to play with Alex when he touched his arm. He showed good voice control when he spoke to Alex who was nearby and spoke clearly to Jamie when he was a short distance away. He also used his voice loudly to express anger. He showed good use of language as he constructed sentences correctly and used a wide vocabulary. For example, 'We can make big holes for dinosaurs!'

He used adjectives correctly, such as 'big', 'deep', 'huge'.

He used prepositions correctly, e.g. 'behind', 'in'.

He used verbs correctly such as 'hiding', 'play', 'make'.

He used present, past and future tenses correctly, e.g. 'He's hiding', 'buried' and 'we can make'. 'Past, present and future tenses are used more often' (Meggitt *et al.*, 2011, p.59).

Social development:

Tom showed social skills when he interacted with Alex and opened the conversation. He seemed to have some understanding of friendship when he shouted: 'I'll never be your friend ever now!' in response to the push. He showed the ability to interact positively with Jamie. 'Enjoys the company of others; learns to play with other children, not just alongside them' (Kamen, 2011, p.17). He showed awareness of the adult in the room when he moved towards Ms K. He showed some understanding of manners when he said 'please'. He showed the ability to use language to resolve the conflict with Alex rather than fighting. 'Uses language to communicate more and more effectively with others' (Kamen, 2011, p.17).

Emotional development:

Tom showed pleasure when he smiled at Alex and Jamie. He showed anger when he used his voice to shout at Alex in response to the push. 'Begins to use language to express feelings and wishes' (Kamen, 2011, p.18). He showed the ability to control his emotions when he resisted crying and did not push Alex in retaliation. He showed confidence when he was not put off by Alex's rejection and approached Jamie instead. He showed independence when he did not ask the teacher to intervene.

Intellectual development:

Tom showed good use of imagination and some knowledge of the world when he referred to dinosaurs. For example 'We can make big holes for dinosaurs!' The child understands ideas such as 'big' and 'small' (Meggitt *et al.*, 2011, p.59). He may have demonstrated memory skills when he talked about *Jurassic Park*. He showed observational skills when he looked around the room for a friend to play with.

Physical development:

He showed different locomotion skills when he walked towards Alex and skipped with Jamie. He showed balance when he did not fall over when pushed forcefully by Alex. 'A sense of balance is developing – the child may be able to walk along a line' (Meggitt *et al.*, 2011, p.59).

Personal learning:

From doing this observation I have learned that this particular method of observing children (written narrative) was an appropriate method of observing a young child's communication skills while playing. It was a straightforward method to use and as only one child was being observed it was quite easy to record everything the child said and did in a 5-minute period.

Recommendations:

To encourage and extend Tom's communication skills, I suggest providing plenty of opportunities for Tom to play with other children, such as imaginative play: role play in the home corner, dressing-up activities, dolls and puppets, small world toys.

References/bibliography:

Kamen, T. (2011) *Teaching Assistant's Handbook Level 3: Supporting Teaching and Learning in Schools*. London: Hodder Education.

Meggitt, C. *et al.* (2011) *CACHE Level 3 Diploma: Children and Young People's Workforce – Early Learning and Child Care*. London: Hodder Education.

Table 4.2 Example of written narrative observation including evaluation

 Activity

1. Have a go at doing an observation using **written narrative**. For example, observe a young child playing and focus on the child's physical skills (e.g. gross motor skills, fine motor skills, co-ordination), as this should be fairly straightforward.
2. Include the following information in your assessment:
   - The type and location of the activity observed (e.g. sand and water play in the outdoor area or dressing up in the home corner).
   - The intended learning goals/objectives for the child, e.g. physical skills.
   - The actual learning and development skills across all areas (especially the three prime areas) as demonstrated by the child.
   - The child's communication skills and behaviour during the activity.
   - Suggestions for extending the child's development and learning.
3. Use relevant sections from this book (and other childcare books) to help you with your assessment. Remember your setting's guidelines for child observations, e.g. ensure you have the necessary permissions to carry out the observation and that you maintain any confidentiality requirements.

Running record

Running records are written descriptions of the child's behaviour. They offer immediate records of what the child says or does in sequence. There are various ways you can make running records: by using words; audiotapes; videos; photographs; sketches; socio-grams; diagrams. This type of record can help you and others to reflect on the past, focus on the present and plan for the future.

This is a popular method that can provide a sound foundation in observing from which you can branch out into alternative methods (Harding & Meldon-Smith, 2001, p.60).

 Key Term

Running record: a written description of a child's behaviour – what the child says or does is in sequence.

Diaries

Diaries can be used, probably on a daily basis, as you carry out your work with children. You can record developmental changes, group or individual changes. This method may be a useful way of collecting detailed information over a period of time. Using a diary ensures that the observation takes only the child into account but also more fully the context of the child's environment. It may therefore contain features of other methods, such as anecdotal records and running records. The diary method is to be chosen with care, because of the time commitment necessary. Particular care must be taken to ensure accurate and objective observations are recorded. This method of recording can easily become subjective, biased and unreliable (Harding & Meldon-Smith, 2001, p.55).

Target child

A target child observation (also known as a coded observation) focuses on one child by collecting data on a prepared record sheet using abbreviations or codes (see Tables 4.3a and 4.3b). This method involves writing down what the child does in each minute in the activity column. You should write down exactly what happens without adding your interpretation. You should also note what the activity is and any material or equipment used, as well as whether other children or adults are present. Write down what the child says and what other children or adults say to the child for each minute in the language column. You probably will not be able to write down every word spoken (unless you use shorthand), so just record the main comments. If interrupted during the observation just note 'interruption' on the record sheet, and resume when possible. When you are finished make a note of what the child does next so that you can make sense of what the child was doing at the end of the observation (Harding & Meldon-Smith, 2001, pp.54–5).

 Key Term

Target child observation: also known as coded observation, this focuses on one child by collecting data on a prepared record sheet using abbreviations or codes.

Minutes	Activity	Language	Task	Social
1	TC is threading beads on to a lace	Sings to herself	MAN	SOL
2	TC reaches out to get more beads	TC sp. A: asks for help in reaching the bead box	MAN	PAIR

Minutes	Activity	Language	Task	Social
3	TC continues to thread beads as another two children come to the table	TC sp. A&C: tells them what she is making. A responds positively	MAN	SG
4	TC puts lace around her neck and tries to fasten it to make necklace	A sp. TC: asks if she thinks that it is long enough. TC nods TC sp. A: asks adult to fasten the lace	MAN	SG
5	TC moves away from table and goes to wash her hands for snack time	A sp. LG: that it is time to tidy up	DA	SOL

Table 4.3a Target child

General codes	Task codes	Social codes
TC = target child	MAN = manipulation	SOL = solitary
A = adult	DA = domestic activity, e.g. routines	PAIR = 2 people together
C = other child		SG = small group
sp. = speaks to		LG = large group

Table 4.3b Target child key

A full, detailed written record of a child's movements during a predetermined time can offer practitioners a full account of:

- Which specific activities the child has selected.
- Which area(s) of the learning environment he/she has been working in.
- With whom he/she has interacted.
- With whom he/she has spoken.
- Evidence of expressive language used.

While observing a child in this way it is useful to have a watch nearby and to note the time at frequent intervals, clarifying the exact time spent at each activity. As a result of the observations strategies can be implemented to promote changes for the child, the practitioners and/or the setting (Wall, 2006, p.98).

Activity

1. Have a go at doing an observation using the **target child** method. For example, observe a young child playing and focus on the child's social interaction skills (e.g. interaction with adults and/or other children, communication skills, language used).

2. Include the following information in your assessment:
   - The type and location of the activity observed (e.g. playing with small world toys, small construction or jigsaws).
   - The intended learning goals/objectives for the child, e.g. social skills.
   - The actual learning and development skills across all areas (especially the three prime areas) as demonstrated by the child.
   - The child's language and communication skills during the activity.
   - Suggestions for extending the child's development and learning.

3. Use relevant sections from this book (and other childcare books) to help you with your assessment. Remember your setting's guidelines for child observations, e.g. ensure you have the necessary permissions to carry out the observation and that you maintain any confidentiality requirements.

Time sample

A time sample involves the observer making a note of the child's actions and interactions at regular intervals over a set period of time. Time sampling can be used to record an individual or group of children. Recording is not continuous but is carried out at regular intervals, such as every 15 minutes throughout the day or session, as appropriate. Time samples can be used to look at a child's specific activity or behaviour, and can be recorded on a prepared chart or produced as a written description.

 Key Term

Time sample: an observer makes notes of a child's or group of children's actions and interactions at regular intervals over a set period of time.

Time	Activity	Comments
9:00 a.m.	Arrives in the Reception class	Tom holds tightly on to his mum's hand and does not reply when the teacher speaks to him. Follows instruction to hang up his coat on his peg. Starts to cry as Mum tells him she is leaving. Mum leaves and Tom runs to the window to watch her. Does not speak to the teacher when she approaches him.
9:15 a.m.	Sitting on the carpet	Tom is still crying quietly but nods, avoiding eye contact, when the teacher calls his name on the register.

Time	Activity	Comments
9:30 a.m.	Writing table with a small group	Tom is with three other children sitting at the writing table. They are drawing pictures and writing about what they did on Bank Holiday Monday. One child asks Tom to pass her a purple crayon, so Tom stretches across with his right hand and gives the purple crayon to the other child, but does not speak and again avoids eye contact.
9:45 a.m.	Book corner	Tom is in the book corner alone. The teacher asks Tom if he would like to read a story with her. He looks down and shakes his head to indicate no.

Table 4.4 Time sample

A practitioner can use time sampling to monitor concerns about a child's lack of interactions with others, for example. The child may be observed every 10 minutes throughout a session of 3 hours. At each 10 minute interval, the observer will note exactly where the child is in the room, any interactions with others, and the nature of the interactions. The outcomes of such an observation will clarify for the practitioner (and others) the amount of time spent interacting with others, and action can be considered, such as encouraging the child's increased involvement in activities with others, starting with one-to-one, then pairs, then small group.

Time sampling is also useful to investigate aspects of the learning environment. For example, practitioners at the setting may be concerned about the lack of use made of the book corner and a time sampling approach can be used to note if there are children using the book corner or not at pre-set intervals. If results indicate that the book corner is used for a minimum amount of session time, then the staff can devise ways to make alterations to encourage greater usage. Similarly, if the quality of language used in the book corner is a concern, then this can be recorded at the same time intervals (Wall, 2006, p.96).

 Activity

1. Have a go at doing an observation using **time sampling**. For example, observe how a young child copes with the hand-over routine at the start of the day/session.
2. Include the following information in your assessment:
   - The child's reactions to and interaction with adults and/or other children, as well as any language used.
   - Suggestions for encouraging the child's development and learning, e.g. helping them to cope with the settling-in routine.
3. Use relevant sections from this book (and other childcare books) to help you with your assessment. Remember your setting's guidelines for child observations, e.g. ensure you have the necessary permissions to carry out the observation and that you maintain any confidentiality requirements.

Event sample

Event samples are similar to time samples but data is not recorded at fixed times. The frequency of the event determines the amount of information gathered. This observation technique is often used when there are concerns about a child, such as behaviour or emotional difficulties. This technique can also be used to record other events, however, such as how frequently a young child uses a transition object, such as a dummy. Event sampling enables the practitioner to record when the event occurred, what led up to the event, how long the event lasted, how adult(s) responded to the event. This information can help the practitioner to work out what triggers the event in order to devise and implement appropriate strategies to change or modify the child's behaviour. This data is usually recorded on a chart, but the way in which the chart is set out will depend on the information required to meet the aim of the observation. For example:

Event	Date and time	Situation	Comment
1	02/02/12 8:00 a.m.	Enters nursery with Mum	Has dummy in mouth as Mum hands Tom to his key person.
2	02/02/12 9:15 a.m.	On the carpet playing with key person	Tom has his dummy in his hand. 'Please may I have that?' asks the adult. Tom shakes his head and puts the dummy in his mouth.
3	02/02/12 9:45 a.m.	In the quiet room	Tom has his dummy in his mouth as the key person lies him down for morning nap.
4	02/02/12 10:00 a.m.	In the quiet room	The key person takes the dummy out of Tom's mouth. He immediately wakes up and cries. Key person puts back dummy and Tom goes back to sleep.

Table 4.5 Event sample

 Key Term

Event sample: an observer makes notes on a child's/children's actions and interactions. There is no fixed time at which these notes are made; the frequency of the event determines the amount of information gathered.

Event sampling (also known as frequency sampling) is useful when practitioners wish to clarify their understanding of a specific event, as it records the frequency of an event. As an example, if we are observing a child's unacceptable behaviour, for example hitting another child, the information can be used as a baseline. A programme or strategies can be implemented to reduce this behaviour and possibly encourage an alternative behaviour. Then at a later date the observations can be repeated, hopefully to highlight an improvement in behaviours demonstrated and success of the intervention.

Recording can take the form of a simple tick sheet to indicate the number of times the behaviour occurs, or more details can be included, such as time of day, antecedents, consequences, whether an adult was present and so on (Wall, 2006, p.96).

 Activity

1. Have a go at doing an observation using **event sampling**. For example, observe and record a young child during specific events or when demonstrating certain behaviour (e.g. observe and record the number of times the target behaviour occurs, when it occurs and how long it lasts).
2. Include the following information in your assessment:
   - The type and location of the routines/activities observed (e.g. meal/snack time, story time, circle time, playing games or other co-operative activity).
   - The child's behaviour during the activity.
   - The child's communication skills.
   - How the adult responds to the child's behaviour.
   - How the other children respond to the child's behaviour.
   - Suggestions on how to monitor the child's behaviour and promote more positive behaviour in the future.
3. Use relevant sections from this book (and other childcare books) to help you with your assessment. Remember your setting's guidelines for child observations, e.g. ensure you have the necessary permissions to carry out the observation and that you maintain any confidentiality requirements.

Checklist

Checklists are often the preferred choice for early years practitioners and are viewed by some as easier to implement and interpret. Certain considerations should be reflected upon, however, before relying on checklists for assessment evidence.

1. Checklists only offer a snapshot picture of what a child can do, on that day and at that particular time, and tend to note achieved milestones.
2. For children experiencing complex special needs, by nature of the large gaps between skills given on the checklist, they equally represent the skills a child has not mastered. If the checklists do not cover every physical skill, for example, then only those checked can be commented on.
3. A checklist may indicate that a child can hop, jump, run and catch a large ball at 2 metres, but may not show whether the child can pedal a tricycle. Caution should therefore be employed in the interpretation of outcomes if a thorough understanding of a child's development is required as opposed to a snapshot picture.
4. Within the philosophy of holistic provision for young children, checklists can be interpreted as more like a preordained assessment check that clearly does not fit with the holistic philosophy.
5. Checklists are created around a sequential approach to development and assume that all children will progress through the defined stages in much the same systematic order. Practitioners working with children in the early years (especially those with special needs) will be aware that not all children progress this way.
6. Developmental checklists are used in many early years settings, for example baseline assessments.

7. Usually presented in tabular form (see Table 4.6), checklists are generally easy to interpret and therefore accessible to all, but they can also be represented pictorially so the children themselves can be involved in recording their own progress (see Figure 4.3).

8. Strategies to support children who need to develop particular skills further can be devised and implemented using the evidence from the checklists, which can be updated regularly as part of an ongoing monitoring process.

(Wall, 2006, p.102–3)

Name	Walking	Running	Jumping	Climbing	Skipping	Hopping	Galloping	Balancing
Shafik	c	c	c	e	e	e	e	e
Sukhvinder	c	c	c	c	e	e	e	c
Ruth	c	c	c	e	e	c	e	e
Tom	c	c	c	c	e	e	e	c

Table 4.6 Example of a tabular checklist (c = competent at skill, e = emerging skill)

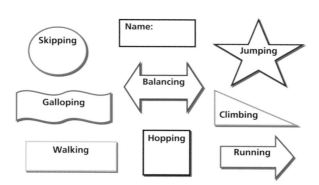

Figure 4.3 Example of a pictorial checklist

Some local authorities may have their own checklists, either self-created or taken from a standardised checklist, for use within all registered early years settings or within special needs settings. Portage workers base all their work on the portage developmental checklists covering all skill areas and breaking down tasks into achievable steps to ensure success. Health visitors and speech and language therapists will use their own specific checklists or screening tools to monitor children's progress. Mortimer (2008) has devised the Playladders checklists, originally created for use in early years settings and using existing checklists as a foundation. They are designed to avoid the developmental checklist approach in favour of approaching observation and assessment from the realities of children's activities (Wall, 2006, p.104).

Mortimer summarises the Playladder process:

'Early years educators are encouraged to play alongside the child as part of their regular activities within a group of children. By observing how a child is playing, it becomes easy to visualise and record the stage on the Playladder later, once the children have left. Play thus proceeds uninterrupted by the assessment and recording. Once the play behaviour is recorded on the checklist, a "next step on the ladder" is suggested, and this new skill can be encouraged or taught at a future play session.'

(Mortimer, 2001, p.125)

Activity

Give examples of the checklists used within your setting.

Graphs and charts

Graphs and charts are not really observation methods; they are actually ways of representing the data collected during observations. Bar graphs and pie charts are pictorial representations of collected data and are constructed after the observation(s).

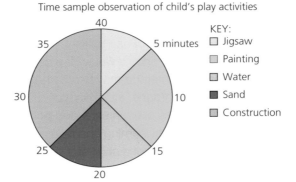

Time sample observation of child's play activities

KEY:
☐ Jigsaw
☐ Painting
☐ Water
■ Sand
☐ Construction

Figure 4.4 Example of a pie chart

Graphs and charts provide clear, accessible information about groups of children, but can also provide information about individual children, such as how long a child is engaged in different play activities.

Activity

1. Have a go at using a **pie chart** to represent the data collected from an observation. For example, observe a young child playing and focus on the child's play preferences (e.g. how long the child participated in each self-chosen play activity).
2. Include the following information in your assessment:
    *   The type and location of each activity observed (e.g. jigsaw in the quiet area, painting in the 'messy' area, sand/water play or construction in the outdoor area).
    *   The intended learning goals/objectives for the child, e.g. concentration levels.
    *   The actual learning and development skills across all areas (especially the three prime areas) as demonstrated by the child.
    *   The child's play preferences and engagement in each activity.
    *   Suggestions for using the child's play preferences to encourage and extend the child's development and learning.
3. Use relevant sections from this book (and other childcare books) to help you with your assessment. Remember your setting's guidelines for child observations, e.g. ensure you have the necessary permissions to carry out the observation and that you maintain any confidentiality requirements.

Longitudinal

A longitudinal study involves carrying out regular observations over a long period of time, e.g. observing a child's development and progress over a few weeks, months or even years. This method is very useful for observing babies and very young children (whose rapidly changing developmental needs require careful monitoring to ensure appropriate practice), as well as children with special needs where long-term support strategies are necessary.

Key Term

Longitudinal study: carrying out regular observations over a long period of time, for example observing a child's development and progress over a few weeks, months or even years.

While studying an early years or childcare course, students are often required to carry out observations, using different observation skills to undertake a longitudinal study of a young child. An example of this type of assignment includes observing a 1- to 2-year-old within the context of a family environment, once a week for a period of 6 to 8 weeks. Each week a different observation and/or assessment method may be used, including the following: checklist; written narrative; time sample; photographs, etc. This type of long-term study enables the student to follow the same child's progress over an extended period of time to gain an in-depth understanding of the nature of observational learning and its use in assessment. This allows the student to learn about developmental patterns of a child of a specific age and relate such patterns to developmental theories such as those of Piaget, Vygotsky and Bruner.

When observing a baby or very young child (as part of a longitudinal study) you will be taking a very detailed look at aspects of development that you might take for granted in an older child. In each observation you should take note of the following:

- The position of the baby (e.g. position of head, arms and legs while lying on back or tummy).
- What the baby's eyes are doing (e.g. open or closed, focusing, following movement, looking towards light and/or sound).
- The baby's facial expressions including lip and tongue movements.
- How the baby moves arms, hands and fingers, legs, feet and toes (including reaching out to grasp objects and how the baby is able to hold things).
- The baby's early attempts at language and communication (e.g. what sounds the baby makes, when and to whom the sounds are made).

Each observation in a longitudinal study should include an update on the child's development since the previous observation. For example: changes in weight and height; changes in feeding pattern; all round developmental progress (SPICE); relevant health matters, including immunisation; changes in family situation; any other important changes since the last observation.

 Activity

1. If possible, have a go at doing a **longitudinal study** of a baby or very young child. For example, observe a baby once a week for several months and focus on the all round development of the baby during daily routines and activities.
2. Include the following information in your assessment:
   - The type and location of each routine/activity observed (e.g. feeding in the kitchen/dining area, nappy changing or bathing in the bathroom, playing with adult in the garden or outdoor play area, communicating with adult in the living room or indoor play area).
   - The intended learning goals/objectives for the baby.
   - The actual learning and development skills across all areas (especially the three prime areas) as demonstrated by the baby.
   - Suggestions to encourage and extend the baby's development and learning.
3. Use relevant sections from this book (and other childcare books) to help you with your assessment. Remember your setting's guidelines for child observations, e.g. ensure you have the necessary permissions to carry out the observation and that you maintain any confidentiality requirements.

Cross-sectional

The cross-sectional method of observation is often used to compare developmental levels at various ages or backgrounds. Many children at different ages are studied in groups according to their age, and the results on the same sets of measures are compared for the groups. For example, the approximate age at which a very young child can be expected to roll over, crawl, pull self up to a standing position, and walk unaided, can be determined by observing the behaviour of groups of children from birth until the age of about 18 months. As part of cross-sectional observations practitioners may study a group of 1-month-old babies and a different group of babies at every month of age thereafter.

 Key Term

Cross-sectional observation: method of observation used to compare developmental levels at various ages or backgrounds.

 Activity

Find out more about cross-sectional observations. You could start by looking at the online article 'Methods of Studying Children – Longitudinal Versus Cross-sectional Studies' – see **http://social.jrank.org/pages/411/Methods-Studying-Children-Longitudinal-versus-Cross-Sectional-Studies.html**

Structured recording system

The structured recording system method involves observing and recording for a specific reason, e.g. capabilities of a child on entry to school or to do a specific task, such as draw a person. The method uses pre-printed sheets that can be completed by all significant people, e.g. the child, their parents, practitioners from current/previous setting. Examples include All About Me record sheets before starting Reception; reading records; forms identifying areas of learning and development in the EYFS (see Chapter 5 in this book). These forms can organise your thoughts and help you decide how best to identify areas in which the child's development is as expected, as well as those where further encouragement or more support may be required.

 Key Term

Structured recording system: observing and recording for a specific reason (for example a child's ability to complete a specific task such as drawing a person) using pre-printed sheets.

Communication and Language Observation
Child's name: *Thomas Jennings* Date: *31 October 2012*

Time of Observation	09:30	10:00	10:30	11:00	11:30	12:00
Participation in activity						
Child alone and not involved in any activity	✓					
Child alone but watches others						
Child absorbed in some activity alone		✓	✓			
Child follows own activity but aware of others				✓		
Child participates in a group					✓	✓
Talk with others						
No talk observed	✓					
Child plays and talks to self, not aware of others		✓	✓			
Child listens to others but not talking						✓
Child talks to others but no responses required				✓		
Child initiates conversation and seeks response						
Child directs behaviour of others						
Child directed by another					✓	
Talk with adults						
Initiates conversation with adult						
Responds when approached by adult					✓	
Maintains a conversation easily						
Maintains a conversation with difficulty						
Contributes when with adult (in a group)						

Communication and Language Observation	
Child's name: *Thomas Jennings*	*Date: 31 October 2012*
General behaviour characteristics: Any particular features of behaviour that emerge (e.g. friendly, confident, aggressive, dominant, shy, shows lack of concentration, etc.)	*Shy.* *Good concentration on activity he found interesting.*
Summary of observed behaviour: *Tom appeared very shy and reluctant to participate in activities until he became absorbed in one activity that held his attention for some time. He was aware of other children but did not join in with their play or interact with them. He showed non-verbal communication when he nodded to the adult who asked him to join a small group activity.*	

Table 4.7 Example of a structured recording system (adapted from *Listening to Children Talking* by Joan Tough, 1976, p.42)

 A *Activity*

Give examples of the structured recording systems used in your setting.

Participant observation

Many of the observations carried out in early years settings are called 'participant observations', and are carried out while practitioners are playing and working with the children. Participant observations involve noting down any significant things you see the children doing or saying when you are working with them in any part of your setting at any time of the day; usually the notes you make will be short and quickly done (Hutchin, 1999, p.44). Many practitioners use sticky notes to jot down brief observations, and this is a practical way to record information. You will need to write enough information so that anyone else reading it can understand.

 K Key Term

Participant observation: enabling researchers to learn about the activities of the children under study in the natural setting through observing and participating in those activities.

It might be difficult sometimes for the key person to be the observer in a planned observation, when close and individual attention is required if children require a high degree of involvement or if you are a childminder; so practitioners usually observe the child they are with as a participant in the activity. Of course this means you cannot easily assess the quality of your own interactions with the child and therefore observations carried out by another person do remain important from time to time (DfE, 2007, p.3).

Observing groups

Observing more than one child usually means that you will need to share out your attention between the children. It does not mean that you have to write more, but you will have to be very focused in your watching and listening. Think carefully about your aims and concentrate only on those particular aims. For example, it could be that your aims were to observe the interaction between the children and to know their use of language (Harding & Meldon-Smith, 2001, p.36).

Socio-grams

A socio-gram can be used to develop a greater understanding of a child's social interactions. Observations may be carried out for a set period of time to note, for example, who the child shared time with, the nature of the interactions and what verbal interactions took place. Again this could be represented graphically if desired and even reflect gender relationships or the type of play the child was involved in (see Figure 4.5). While a socio-gram can clearly focus on one particular area of development, practitioners should note that children's friendships and favoured playmates can fluctuate on a fairly regular basis and this should be reflected in any interpretation of the data (Wall, 2006, p.101).

A child's level of social interaction during play activities depends on: the individual child; the child's previous experiences of play; the play activity itself; the social context, e.g. the setting and other people present. Children go through a recognised sequence of social play (see Table 4.8). Younger children tend to engage in more solitary or parallel play activities because they are more egocentric; older children are capable of more co-operative play activities as they can take turns, share play equipment and follow rules more easily. There will be times when quite young children can be engaged happily in play activities with some interaction with other children (associative play) such as dressing up, home corner, doing jigsaws, simple construction or painting. There will be occasions when older children become engrossed in solitary or parallel play activities with no interaction with other children, e.g. doing detailed drawings and paintings, building intricate constructions that require complete concentration to the exclusion of everyone else.

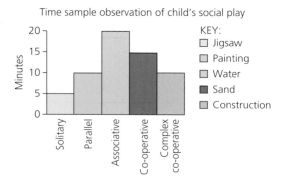

Figure 4.5 Socio-gram showing types of social play

Type of social play	What it means
Solitary play	Child playing alone
Parallel play	Child playing alongside other children without interaction
Associative play	Child playing alongside other children with limited interaction

 *Activity*

1. Have a go at doing an observation using **audio/video recording**. For example, using audio or video recording equipment to observe a young child's use of language.
2. Include the following information in your assessment:
   - The type and location of the activity observed (e.g. playing in the home corner or sharing a story in the book corner).
   - The intended learning goals/objectives for the child, e.g. language skills.
   - The actual learning and development skills across all areas (especially the three prime areas) as demonstrated by the child.
   - The child's use of language and communication skills.
   - Suggestions to encourage and extend the child's development and learning.
3. Use relevant sections from this book (and other childcare books) to help you with your assessment. Remember your setting's guidelines for child observations, e.g. ensure you have the necessary permissions to carry out the observation and that you maintain any confidentiality requirements.

Comparison of methods

The results of child observations can have a huge impact on practice. For example, a child's angry outbursts were observed by event sampling, but in addition to recording the number of times the child was hitting out at others, what preceded the outbursts was also noted. It became clear that the child reacted this way when the group was asked to tidy up and the child was in the middle of a task or project, such as building a garage from bricks, and another child began clearing the equipment away. The strategy that supported this child was to speak to him 5 minutes before tidying up time and decide how to store or protect his work until later, if not finished. Incidents of hitting out reduced dramatically. A significant discovery was made through the observational process and the learning environment was successfully adapted to suit this child's individual needs with very little effort from anyone.

Time sampling and event sampling are both relatively straightforward to undertake and give precise data to work with. Finding the time to complete observations within a busy setting may not be so easy, however, as additional staff may need to be brought in to cover. In addition it is not easy to remain detached from the children and focus solely on the observations in hand and the children themselves may make it difficult by constantly asking you to help or support them, as you would usually do during the session. Children are not used to staff members sitting on the perimeter of the room and writing, instead of playing and working with them (Wall, 2006, pp.97–8).

Uses in different situations

It is important to choose an appropriate method when observing children in order to achieve accurate results that will then inform future planning. Consider these questions:

- Does the method encourage parental contribution?
- Does the method allow the child to contribute?

- Is the format of the methods suitable for all children, whatever their special learning needs or abilities?
- Is the method sensitive to the cultural heritage and variety of languages of the children and their families?
- Is the method appropriate for the working environment?

(Harding & Meldon-Smith, 2001, p.44)

For example, event/frequent sampling can be very useful for observing behaviours that occur infrequently, especially when used in combination with different recording methods. This approach basically involves the observer recording on a checklist each time the child performs a specific action or exhibits a certain type of behaviour. It is the observer who decides which key behaviours constitute the event that has been targeted. An example of an event sample that may be recorded using this method includes observing each time a child exhibits signs of aggressive behaviour and any causal factors. The knowledge gained from this observation would then likely be helpful in terms of identifying possible triggers (Le Page, 2010b).

 Activity

Compare the different methods of observation. Think about which methods would be most appropriate to use in different situations. For example, suggest an appropriate method for each of the following and give reasons for your chosen methods:

- To observe a group of children's social development, e.g. social interaction.
- To observe a group of children's physical development, e.g. co-ordination.
- To observe a child's intellectual development, e.g. concentration levels.
- To observe a child's communication and language development, e.g. listening.
- To observe a child's emotional development, e.g. coping with transitions.

Advantages and weaknesses

Effective practitioners should be able to identify the advantages and weaknesses of different observation methods (see Table 4.9).

 Activity

Think about the methods of observation used in your setting. Focus on the four observation methods you use the most frequently and identify each method's advantages and disadvantages.

Limitations with methods

One of the main limitations of observation methods is that they can be very time consuming and resource intensive. A fundamental potential limitation of all observation is that it is susceptible to observer bias; that is, subjective bias on the part of the observer that can undermine the reliability and the validity of the information gathered. This can be because the observer records not what

Observation method	Advantages	Weaknesses
Verbatim reporting	• Provides a word-for-word record of what has been said • Can record a variety of conversations: between two or more children, between a child and an adult, or between children and an adult • Allows observer to gain insights into a child's language development as you can listen repeatedly to specific words or phrases	• Takes time to transcribe recorded conversations
Written narrative	• A good method to start with • Little preparation • Easy to learn • Straightforward to use	• Result may be repetitious • Need to learn how to write down key points • May be lengthy
Target child	• Provides a focused example of a child's behaviour • Can be used for a range of different purposes, such as activities over a specific period of time, social interaction, language and communication • Is relatively clear and easy to use • Helps to focus on language, social interaction and activities of the child being observed	• Need to learn and practise the use of each code before putting it into practice • Need to be familiar with the codes and need good concentration skills • The information or data can be limited • Must be pre-planned and use a specially prepared chart, therefore cannot be used for spontaneous observations
Time sample	• Economical and efficient • An accurate picture about what a child is doing can be built up • One aspect (e.g. of behaviour) can be studied • Observations can be recorded over a long period of time • Different time intervals can be selected to best suit the purpose of the observation • Simple and easy to record • Can be used for individuals and groups of children • No restrictions on the types of behaviour to be observed • Allows for multiple recording techniques	• Pre-arranged schedule must be adhered to (if not your own preferences start to emerge!) • If one aspect of behaviour is to be observed it is difficult to ignore everything else • Can forget to record data at the correct time, so good timekeeping skills are needed • May need to involve other adults if the recording is over more than one day or session • May not record something significant that the child does if it occurs outside of timed record samples

(Continued)

Observation method	Advantages	Weaknesses
Event sample	• Useful for recording particular circumstances or positive or negative behaviour • Useful as a basis for forward planning • Useful to observe one child • Simple and easy to use • Builds up a picture of a specific behaviour or concern	• Difficult to observe a group of children • Need a prepared chart and therefore cannot be spontaneous • May require input from other adults
Checklist	• A quick way to identify developmental progress • May identify strengths and weaknesses • May identify exceptional ability • Easy technique to learn • Recording is easy • Can be used to record the activities of a whole group or an individual child • Efficient method to observe in a wide range of contexts, especially where there are major time restrictions	• Results may be relied on in isolation • Advanced and careful planning is necessary to decide which information needs to be sought • Best results achieved if a good knowledge of the child exists • Best results achieved if adult is familiar to the child • Contain predefined categories or aspects of behaviour (child may be unable to meet these targets) • Lack of detail – checklists only provide 'yes' or 'no' answers
Graphs and charts	• Information gathered is clearly presented • Efficient method • Provides good information about groups of children	• Does not tend to provide sufficient information for individual children
Longitudinal	• Provides an opportunity for a general understanding of development	• Time burden can be too great • Unforeseen circumstances may interrupt the study
Cross-sectional	• Less time consuming than longitudinal • Allows researchers to compare many different variables at the same time • Useful initial studies to generate hypotheses	• May not provide clear evidence for cause and effect relationships • Does not provide a clear natural progression of development (do not know what happens before or after the snapshot is taken)

Observation method	Advantages	Weaknesses
Photographs and audio or video recording	<ul><li>Have a range of uses</li><li>May help to confirm findings obtained through other observational methods as tends to be unbiased</li><li>Straightforward to use</li></ul>	<ul><li>Not possible to retain anonymity</li><li>Evaluation should only be undertaken alongside other observational recordings</li><li>May be lengthy</li></ul>
Mapping	<ul><li>Helps identify child's/children's needs, by watching their use of space</li><li>Helps identify accessibility of equipment and how frequently used</li><li>Helps identify safety issues in the space used by the children</li></ul>	<ul><li>Needs to be used with other methods of observing for in-depth analysis</li><li>Results may be of limited use</li></ul>

Table 4.9 Advantages and weaknesses of different observation methods (adapted from Harding & Meldon-Smith, 2001)

actually happened, but what they either wanted to see, expected to see, or just thought they saw. Accurate observations depend on the experience of the practitioner observer; the more you carry out observations the better you will become at doing them, especially when sharing and comparing findings with other practitioners who work with and observe the same children.

Another potential limitation of observation is that the observer's presence may influence the behaviour of those being observed. In order to avoid or minimise this, methods of observation sometimes attempt to be as unobtrusive as possible. However, as observation should be a part of everyday practice within the setting, children will become so used to it that they carry on their activities as usual; being regularly observed will not be seen as out of the ordinary, just as everyday occurrences.

In addition, observing any social group can be difficult (especially in a busy Reception classroom with a large number of children and few adults) as many things are often happening at the same time. In such situations it is impossible for the practitioner to observe (and record) everyone, and decisions have to be made about who to observe and when to observe them; this may mean that significant evidence may be missed, leading to invalid interpretations of the group's behaviour.

Memory

As a practitioner, you cannot simply trust your powers of observation and memory. You might think that you are able to retain loads of information in your head and that it's not necessary to make notes. Even with a brilliant memory, however, you will still lose some of the details of what you have observed, especially if you are responsible for monitoring the progress of lots of children. It is important to note things down as they happen or as soon as possible after. For example using field notes, sticky notes or a diary to jot down important information and writing up more detailed observations at the end of the day as required.

It is also important that your observations (and subsequent assessments) are accessible to other workers when you are not available. Obviously it takes time to develop an effective observation and record keeping system (see detailed information in Chapter 3).

Unfamiliarity with checklist or structured method

Make sure that you know and understand all the different observation methods used in your setting. Start by concentrating on learning the main observation methods that you are expected to use as part of the formative assessment of the children you work with regularly. Then learn how to use any checklists or structured methods that are part of the summative assessment. The best way to learn observation methods is to practise and keep practising! Use the experiences of more senior practitioners to find out how the best ways to carry out observations in your setting.

Limitations with recording

Doing regular observations should not prevent you from interacting with the children. The time spent recording observations must be balanced against the needs of the children being observed and the requirements of the setting. Keep note taking to a minimum by only recording what you actually **see** and **hear** – any evaluation can be noted later as part of the assessment process. Practitioners who are new to observing may worry about what to do if a child is hurt during the observation. If no other adult is nearby to deal with the situation then you *must* stop the observation immediately and provide appropriate assistance and/or comfort to the child. **Remember, your prime concern must always be the safety and well-being of the child** (Harding & Meldon-Smith, 2001, p.34).

Writing quickly enough

Many students or new practitioners worry about being able to write everything down when observing children. If you have clear aims for your observations this will help you to record only the necessary information rather than attempting too much (Harding & Meldon-Smith, 2001, p.35).

Notes can take several forms when you are observing a child. At its most basic, you can use a system of informal notation on a sticky note to supplement or form the basis of more in-depth notes or records about the child. Using your own form of shorthand gives you a way to jot down impressions quickly and as they occur, to be elaborated on later.

Illegible notes

It is essential that the notes you make during observations are legible. You do not want to take the time and trouble to observe children only to find that you cannot read your own notes! Using your own form of shorthand can also help, using obvious, recognisable abbreviations and key words can help you and others to decipher your notes.

 Activity

Think about the limitations of the methods of observation used in your setting. Suggest practical ways to overcome these limitations.

CHAPTER 5

Observing the areas of learning and development

This chapter provides you with information about observing the areas of learning and development in the EYFS, including:

* Observing and identifying ages/stages of the development of young children
* Observing the three prime areas of learning and development
* Observing the four specific areas of learning and development
* Using observation and assessment to deliver planned and purposeful play.

Introduction

Early years practitioners need a detailed knowledge and understanding of the development of children aged from 0 to 5 years. Related to this understanding is the observation of development in the three prime areas of learning and development (personal, social and emotional development; physical development; communication and language) and the four specific areas of learning and development (literacy; mathematics; understanding the world; expressive arts and design), which facilitates the assessment of individual children in order to promote their development through planned and purposeful play.

Observing and identifying ages/stages of the development of young children

It is more accurate to think in terms of sequences of children's development rather than stages of development. This is because stages refers to development that occurs at **fixed ages**, while sequences indicates development that follows the same basic pattern **but not necessarily at fixed ages**. The developmental charts below *do* indicate specific ages, but only to provide a framework to help you understand the usual pattern of children's development.

 Key Terms

Sequences: development following the same basic pattern but not necessarily at fixed ages.

Stages: development that occurs at fixed ages.

The sequence of children's development: 0 to 3 months

Social development

- Cries to communicate needs to others; stops crying to listen to others.
- Responds to smiles from others; responds positively to others, e.g. family members and even friendly strangers unless very upset (when only main caregiver will do!).
- Considers others only in relation to satisfying own needs for food, drink, warmth, sleep, comfort and reassurance.

Physical development

- Sleeps much of the time and grows fast.
- Tries to lift head.
- Starts to kick legs, with movements gradually becoming smoother.
- Starts to wave arms about.
- Begins to hold objects when placed in hand, e.g. an appropriately sized/shaped rattle.
- Grasp reflex diminishes as hand and eye co-ordination begins to develop.
- Enjoys finger play, e.g. simple finger rhymes.
- Becomes more alert when awake.
- Learns to roll from side on to back.
- Sees best at distance of 25cm, then gradually starts watching objects further away.
- Needs opportunities to play and exercise, e.g. soft toys, cloth books and play-mat with different textures and sounds.

Intellectual development

- Recognises parents; concentrates on familiar voices rather than unfamiliar ones.
- Aware of different smells.
- Explores by putting objects in mouth.
- Observes objects that move; responds to bright colours and bold images.
- Stores and recalls information through images.
- Sees everything in relation to self (is egocentric).

Communication and language development

- Recognises familiar voices; stops crying when hears them.
- Aware of other sounds; turns head towards sounds.
- Responds to smiles; moves whole body in response to sound or to attract attention.
- Pauses to listen to others; makes noises as well as crying, e.g. burbling.

Emotional development

- Becomes very attached to parent/carer (usually the mother).
- Experiences extreme emotions, e.g. very scared, very happy or very angry; these moods change in an instant.
- Requires the security and reassurance of familiar routines.
- May be upset by unfamiliar methods of handling and care.

Table 5.1 The sequence of children's development: 0 to 3 months

The sequence of children's development: 3 to 9 months

Social development

- Responds positively to others, especially to familiar people such as family members; by 9 months is very wary of strangers.
- Communicates with others by making noises and participating in 'conversation-like' exchanges; responds to own name.
- Begins to see self as separate from others.

Physical development

- Establishes head control; moves head to follow people and objects.
- Begins to sit with support; sits unsupported from about 6 months.
- Rolls over.
- May begin to crawl, stand and cruise while holding on to furniture (from about 6 months).
- Learns to pull self up to sitting position.
- Begins to use palmar grasp and transfers objects from one hand to the other.
- Develops pincer grasp using thumb and index finger from about 6 months.
- Continues to enjoy finger rhymes.
- Drops things deliberately and searches for hidden/dropped objects (from about 8 months).
- Puts objects into containers and takes them out.
- Enjoys water play in the bath.
- Needs opportunities for play and exercise, including soft toys, board books, bricks, containers, activity centres, etc.

Intellectual development

- Knows individuals and recognises familiar faces.
- Recognises certain sounds and objects.
- Shows interest in everything, especially toys and books.
- Concentrates on well-defined objects and follows direction of moving objects.
- Anticipates familiar actions and enjoys games such as 'peep-po'.
- Searches for hidden or dropped objects (from about 8 months).
- Observes what happens at home and when out and about.
- Explores immediate environment once mobile.
- Processes information through images.
- Enjoys water play in the bath.
- Sees everything in relation to self (is still egocentric).

Communication and language development

- Responds with smiles.
- Recognises family names, but cannot say them.
- Enjoys looking at pictures and books.
- Even more responsive to voices and music.
- Participates in simple games, e.g. 'peep-po'; tries to imitate sounds, e.g. during rhymes.
- Starts babbling; uses single syllable sounds, e.g. 'daa', 'baa' and 'maa'.
- From about 7 months uses two syllable sounds, e.g. 'daada', 'baaba', 'maama'.
- Shouts to attract attention.

(Continued)

Emotional development

- Has strong attachment to parent/carer (usually the mother).
- Develops other attachments to people sees regularly.
- By 6 or 7 months shows clear preferences for familiar adults as can differentiate between individuals.
- Demonstrates strong emotions through body language, gestures and facial expressions.
- Dislikes anger in others and becomes distressed by it.
- Has clear likes and dislikes, e.g. will push away food, drink or toys s/he does not want.

Table 5.2 The sequence of children's development: 3 to 9 months

The sequence of children's development: 9 to 18 months

Social development

- Responds to simple instructions (if wants to!).
- Communicates using (limited) range of recognisable words.
- Shows egocentric behaviour, e.g. expects to be considered first; all toys belong to them.
- Is unintentionally aggressive to other children.

Physical development

- Is now very mobile, e.g. crawls, bottom-shuffles, cruises, walks.
- Starts to go upstairs (with supervision) but has difficulty coming down.
- Needs a safe environment in which to explore as becomes increasingly mobile, e.g. remember safety gates on stairs, etc.
- Throws toys deliberately.
- Watches ball rolling towards self and tries to push it back.
- Has mature pincer grasp and can scribble with crayons.
- Points to objects using index finger.
- Places one (or more) bricks on top of each other to make a small tower.
- Holds a cup and tries to feed self.
- Continues to enjoy finger rhymes plus action songs.
- Needs space, materials and opportunities to play alongside other children.

Intellectual development

- Explores immediate environment using senses, especially sight and touch; has no sense of danger.
- Concentrates more, due to curiosity and increased physical skills, but still has short attention span.
- Follows one-step instructions and/or gestured commands.
- Observes other people closely and tries to imitate their actions.
- Uses 'trial and error' methods when playing with bricks, containers.
- Searches for hidden or dropped objects (aware of object permanence).
- Learns that objects can be grouped together.
- Continues to store and recall information through images.
- Is still egocentric.

The sequence of children's development: 9 to 18 months

Communication and language development

- Continues to imitate sounds; starts jargoning, e.g. joins up syllables so more like 'sentences', such as 'Maama-baaba-daa'.
- Learns to say first real words, usually the names of animals and everyday things.
- Uses gestures to emphasise word meanings.
- Uses vocabulary of between 3 and 20 words.
- Participates in simple finger rhymes; continues to enjoy books.
- Over-extends words, i.e. uses same word to identify similar objects, e.g. all round objects are called 'ball'.

Emotional development

- Likes to get own way; gets very angry when adult says 'No!'.
- Has emotional outbursts ('temper tantrums') when does not get own way or is otherwise frustrated, e.g. unable to do activity because of physical limitations.
- Shows fear in new situations, e.g. attending parent/toddler group, visiting somewhere new such as the farm or nature centre.
- Relies on parent/carer for reassurance and support in new situations.
- Is upset by the distress of other children (even if they caused it).
- Seeks reassurance and contact with familiar adults throughout waking hours.

Table 5.3 The sequence of children's development: 9 to 18 months

The sequence of children's development: 18 months to 2 years

Social development

- Responds positively to others, e.g. plays alongside other children and enjoys games with known adults.
- Communicates more effectively with others; responds to simple instructions.
- Wants to help adults and enjoys imitating their activities.
- May be interested in older children and their activities; imitates these activities.
- May unintentionally disrupt the play of others, e.g. takes toys away to play with by self.
- Becomes very independent, e.g. wants to do things by self.
- Still demonstrates egocentric behaviour; wants own way and says 'No!' a lot.

Physical development

- Starts using potty but has difficulty keeping dry.
- Can feed self.
- Walks well and tries to run but has difficulty stopping.
- Comes downstairs on front with help.
- Learns to push a pedal-less tricycle or sit-and-ride toy with feet.
- Tries to throw ball but has difficulty catching.
- Bends down to pick things up.
- Uses several bricks to make a tower.
- Continues to scribble as fine motor skills improve and can do very simple jigsaw puzzles.
- Enjoys action songs and rhymes.
- Needs space, materials and opportunities to play alongside other children.

(Continued)

The sequence of children's development: 18 months to 2 years

Intellectual development

- Recognises objects from pictures and books.
- Points to desired objects; selects named objects.
- Matches basic colours; starts to match shapes.
- Does very simple puzzles.
- Follows one-step instructions.
- Concentrates for longer, e.g. searching for hidden object, but attention span still quite short.
- Shows lots of curiosity and continues exploring using senses and 'trial and error' methods.
- Processes information through images and increasingly through language too.
- Shows preferences and starts to make choices.
- Is still egocentric.

Communication and language development

- Uses language to gain information, e.g. starts asking 'What dat?'
- Repeats words said by adults.
- Acquires 1–3 words per month; by 2 years has vocabulary of about 200 words.
- Participates in action songs and nursery rhymes; continues to enjoy books and stories.
- Uses telegraphic speech, e.g. speaks in 2–3 word sentences such as 'Daddy go' or 'Milk all gone'.

Emotional development

- Begins to disengage from secure attachment, e.g. wants to do things by self – 'Me do it!'
- Still emotionally dependent on familiar adult(s) but this leads to conflict as need for independence grows.
- Has mood swings, e.g. clingy one moment, then fiercely independent the next.
- Becomes very frustrated when unable/not allowed to do a particular activity, which leads to frequent but short-lived emotional outbursts ('temper tantrums').
- Explores environment; even new situations are less frightening as long as parent/carer is present.

Table 5.4 The sequence of children's development: 18 months to 2 years

The sequence of children's development: 2 to 3 years

Social development

- Continues to enjoy the company of others.
- Wants to please and seeks approval from adults.
- Is still very egocentric and very protective of own possessions; unable to share with other children although may give toy to another child if adult requests it, to please the adult.
- May find group experiences difficult due to this egocentric behaviour.
- Uses language more effectively to communicate with others.

The sequence of children's development: 2 to 3 years

Physical development

- Uses potty and stays dry more reliably.
- Comes downstairs in upright position, one step at a time.
- Starts to climb well on play apparatus.
- Kicks a ball, learns to jump and may learn to somersault.
- Learns to pedal a tricycle.
- Can undress self; tries to dress self but needs help, especially with socks and fastenings.
- Fine motor skills improving; has increased control of crayons and paintbrush; tries to use scissors.
- Enjoys construction activities and can build more complex structures.
- Continues to enjoy action songs and rhymes.
- Needs space, materials and opportunities to play alongside and with other children.

Intellectual development

- Identifies facial features and main body parts.
- Continues to imitate other children and adults.
- Follows two-step instructions.
- Matches more colours and shapes, including puzzles and other matching activities.
- Points to named object in pictures and books.
- Develops understanding of big and small.
- Begins to understand concept of time at basic level, e.g. before/after, today/tomorrow.
- Enjoys imaginative play; able to use symbols in play, e.g. pretend a doll is a real baby.
- Concentrates on intricate tasks such as creative activities or construction, but may still have short attention span, especially if not really interested in the activity.
- Is very pre-occupied with own activities; still egocentric.
- Shows some awareness of right and wrong.
- Processes information through language rather than images.

Communication and language development

- Has vocabulary of about 300 words.
- Uses more adult forms of speech, e.g. sentences now include words such as that, this, here, there, then, but, and.
- Can name main body parts.
- Uses adjectives, e.g. big, small, tall; words referring to relationships, e.g. I, my, you, yours.
- Asks questions to gain more information.
- Sings songs and rhymes; continues to participate in action songs and enjoy books/stories.
- Can deliver simple messages.

Emotional development

- May still rely on parent/carer for reassurance in new situations or when with strangers.
- Still experiences emotional outbursts as independence grows and frustration at own limitations continues, e.g. aggressive towards toys that cannot get to work.
- Begins to understand the feelings of others but own feelings are still the most important.
- Has very limited understanding of other people's pain, e.g. if hits another child.
- Feels curious about environment but has no sense of danger, e.g. that they or other people can be hurt by their actions.

Table 5.5 The sequence of children's development: 2 to 3 years

The sequence of children's development: 3 to 5 years

Social development
- Enjoys the company of others; learns to play with other children, not just alongside them.
- Uses language to communicate more and more effectively with others.
- Develops self-help skills (e.g. dressing self, going to the toilet) as becomes more competent and confident in own abilities.
- Still wants to please and seeks approval from adults.
- Observes closely how others behave and imitates them.
- Still fairly egocentric; may get angry with other children if disrupt play activities or snatch play items required for own play; expects adults to take their side in any dispute.
- Gradually is able to share group possessions at playgroup or nursery.

Physical development
- Usually clean and dry but may have occasional 'accidents'.
- Able to run well – and stop!
- Competent at gross motor skills such as jumping, riding a tricycle, climbing play apparatus, using a swing.
- Throws and catches a ball but is still inaccurate.
- Fine motor skills continue to improve, e.g. can use scissors.
- Continues to enjoy action songs plus simple singing and dancing games.
- Needs space, materials and opportunities to play co-operatively with other children.

Intellectual development
- Learns about basic concepts through play.
- Experiments with colour, shape and texture.
- Recalls a simple sequence of events.
- Follows two- or three-step instructions including positional ones, e.g. 'Please put your ball in the box under the table'.
- Continues to enjoy imaginative and creative play.
- Interested in more complex construction activities.
- Concentrates on more complex activities as attention span increases.
- Plays co-operatively with other children; able to accept and share ideas in group activities.
- Shows some awareness of right and wrong, the needs of others.
- Holds strong opinions about likes and dislikes.
- Processes information using language.

Communication and language development
- Has vocabulary of between 900 and 1,500 words.
- Asks lots of questions.
- Uses language to ask for assistance.
- Talks constantly to people knows well.
- Gives very simple accounts of past events.
- Can say names of colours.
- Begins to vocalise ideas.
- Continues to enjoy books, stories, songs and rhymes.
- Listens to and can follow simple instructions; can deliver verbal messages.

The sequence of children's development: 3 to 5 years

Emotional development

- Less reliant on parent/carer for reassurance in new situations.
- May be jealous of adult attention given to younger sibling or other children in a group.
- Argues with other children but is quick to forgive and forget.
- Has limited awareness of the feelings and needs of others.
- May be quite caring towards others who are distressed.
- Begins to use language to express feelings and wishes.
- Still have emotional outbursts especially when tired, stressed or frustrated.

Table 5.6 The sequence of children's development: 3 to 5 years

 Activity

Investigate developmental charts for under-fives. For example:

- 'Birth to Five Timeline' **http://www.nhs.uk/Tools/Pages/birthtofive.aspx?Tag**
- Child development stages: from birth to 6 years
- Revised Development Matters in the Early Years Foundation Stage (see Further reading).

Outline the sequence of children's development for the age group you currently work with.

Milestones of development

The work of people such as Mary Sheridan provides a useful guide to the milestones of **expected** development, that is, the usual pattern of children's development, or norm. As well as their chronological age, children's development is affected by many other factors, e.g. maturation, social interaction, play opportunities, early learning experiences, special needs.

When observing and assessing young children's development, ensure that you include all the aspects of development you can remember using the mnemonic **SPICE**:

- Social
- Physical
- Intellectual
- Communication and language
- Emotional.

 Key Terms

Milestones: significant skills that children develop in and around certain ages as part of the usual or expected pattern of development.

Norm: the usual pattern or expected level of development/behaviour.

Children with particular requirements

When observing young children it is essential to remember that one of the overarching principles of the EYFS is that **children develop and learn in different ways and at different rates**. The EYFS framework covers the education and care of all children in early years provision, including children with special educational needs and disabilities, and those with English as an additional language. Practitioners must consider whether a child may have a special educational need or disability that requires specialist support. They should link with, and help families to access, relevant services from other agencies as appropriate (DfE, 2012).

Depending on their individual experiences, and any special needs, some children may not have reached the same level of development as their peers. Some children may even be ahead of what is usually expected for children their age. (For more information see Chapter 21 'Supporting disabled children and young people and those with specific requirements' in *CACHE Level 3 Diploma: Children and Young People's Workforce – Early Learning and Child Care*, pp.440–65.)

It is important to distinguish between children who have additional language learning needs and those who also have special educational needs (SEN). It is also important not to underestimate what children can do educationally simply

Figure 5.1 Supporting children with particular requirements

because they are learning English as an additional language (EAL). They should be expected to make progress in their learning at the same rate as other children of the same age. However, some children with EAL may also be assessed as having SEN.

For young children whose home language is not English, practitioners must take reasonable steps to provide opportunities for children to develop and use their home language in play and learning, supporting their language development at home. Practitioners must also ensure that young children have plenty of opportunities to learn and reach a good standard in English language during the EYFS. When assessing communication, language and literacy skills, practitioners must assess children's skills in English. If a child does not have a strong grasp of the English language, practitioners must explore the child's skills in the home language with parents and/or carers, to establish whether there is cause for concern about language delay (DfE, 2012, p.6).

Observing the three prime areas of learning and development

The three prime areas reflect the key skills and capacities all children need to develop and learn effectively. Practitioners working with the youngest children should focus strongly on the three prime areas, which are the basis for successful learning in the other four specific areas. It is expected that the balance will shift towards a more equal focus on all areas of learning as children grow in confidence and ability within the three prime areas. Throughout the early years, if a child's progress in any prime area gives cause for concern, practitioners must discuss this with the child's parents and/or carers and agree how to support the child (DfE, 2012, p.6).

Observing young children's personal, social and emotional development

Observing young children's social and emotional development involves seeing and noting how children behave in everyday situations, how they express feelings and emotions, how they relate to each other and to adults, how confident children are and how they feel about themselves (self-concept).

This helps to identify the social and emotional skills the child already has and those skills that need further encouragement and development. Observation also helps to determine the level of adult interaction needed and when to provide appropriate opportunities to encourage children to behave in socially acceptable ways and to develop positive relationships with other children and adults, as well as increasing their independence and confidence. For example, children aged 18 months to 2 years are emotionally dependent on familiar adults but this can lead to conflict (such as emotional outbursts or 'temper tantrums') as their need for independence grows.

 Key Terms

Self-concept: how children feel about themselves.

Emotional outbursts: uncontrolled expressions of intense emotion, e.g. rage or frustration.

 Activity

- Observe a small group of young children during a play activity. Focus on one child's social and emotional skills, e.g. the child's behaviour, level of social interaction, use of communication skills, use of language to express needs and/or feelings, ability to make choices or decisions, imaginative and creative skills.
- Compare the development of the child you have observed with the expected development for a child of this age, looking at all aspects of the child's development but with particular emphasis on the focus area (e.g. social and emotional skills). Include references to support your comments. Suggest further activities to encourage or extend the child's social and emotional development, including any appropriate resources.

Observing young children's physical development

Observing young children's physical development involves seeing and taking note of how children move about, co-ordinate their movements, use space and large equipment, manipulate and use small equipment. This helps to identify the physical skills the child already has and those skills that need further encouragement and development. Observation also helps to determine the level of adult intervention needed and when to provide appropriate opportunities to encourage risk-taking and children's independence. For example, children aged 9 to 18 months need a safe environment in which to explore as they develop their gross motor skills and co-ordination by becoming increasingly mobile, with constant adult care and supervision.

A Activity

- Observe a young child involved in a physical activity such as using indoor or outdoor play equipment. Focus on the physical skills demonstrated by the child, e.g. gross motor skills, fine motor skills and co-ordination skills.
- Compare the development of the child you observed with the expected development for a child of this age, looking at all aspects of the child's development but with particular emphasis on the focus area (e.g. physical skills). Include references to support your comments. Suggest further activities to encourage or extend the child's physical development, including any appropriate resources.

Observing young children's communication and language development

Observing young children's communication and language development involves seeing and noting how children play and interact with others, as well as how they use language to gain and share new information. This helps to identify the communication skills each child already has and those skills that need further encouragement and development.

Observation also helps to determine the level of adult communication and interaction needed and when to provide appropriate stimulating play opportunities to encourage children to communicate in a variety of ways (non-verbal, speaking and listening, reading and writing). For example, children aged 3 to 9 months start babbling using single syllable sounds (daa, baa, maa) and process information through images. Children aged 5 to 7 years have a good vocabulary of familiar words (about 1,500 to 4,000 words) and can use quite complex sentences, which enable them to store and recall more complex information using language.

A Activity

- Observe a young child involved in a conversation, discussion or circle time. Focus on the verbal and/or non-verbal communication used by the child, the complexity of any language used by the child, how the child interacts with others and how the adult encourages the child to communicate.
- Compare the development of the child you observed with the expected development for a child of this age, looking at all aspects of the child's development but with particular emphasis on the focus area (e.g. communication skills). Include references to support your comments. Suggest further activities to encourage or extend the child's communication and language development, including any appropriate resources.

Observing the four specific areas of learning and development

Observing the four specific areas of learning and development (literacy; mathematics; understanding the world; and expressive arts and design) is very useful for gaining knowledge and understanding of each child's all round development, especially their intellectual development. Observing young children's intellectual development involves seeing and noting how children play, use their imagination, take on the roles of others, concentrate on activities, memorise things, solve problems, pay attention to what is around them and use their senses to gain new information. This helps to identify the intellectual skills the child already has and those skills that need further encouragement and development.

Observation also helps to determine the level of adult communication and interaction needed and when to provide appropriate stimulating play opportunities to encourage children to use a wide range of intellectual abilities (sensory perception, thinking, language and communication, reasoning and problem solving, understanding concepts, memory, concentration, imagination and creativity), including using their senses to explore the world around them and acquire new information.

 Activity

- Observe a child over a short period of time (e.g. regular observations over a week). Each observation should focus on one of the four specific areas of learning and development (literacy; mathematics; understanding the world; expressive arts and design). Focus on the child's intellectual abilities (sensory perception, thinking, language and communication, reasoning and problem solving, understanding concepts, memory, concentration, imagination and creativity).
- Compare the development of the child you observed with the expected development for a child of this age, looking at all aspects of the child's development but with particular emphasis on the focus area (e.g. intellectual skills). Include references to support your comments. Suggest further activities to encourage or extend the child's intellectual development, including any appropriate resources.

Using observation and assessment to deliver planned and purposeful play

The planning and implementing of activities for children should come from your observations and assessments of each child's development and learning, your relationship with each child and your understanding of holistic development and learning. (More information about holistic development can be found in Chapter 5 'Understand child and young person development' in Meggitt *et al.*, 2011, pp.49–66.)

Effective planning is based on each child's individual needs, abilities and interests; this is why accurate observations and assessments are so important. Following your observation and assessment of children's development, learning and/or behaviour, your recommendations can provide the basis for planning appropriate activities to encourage and extend each child's skills in the seven areas of learning and development.

Practitioners support children's learning and development through skilfully intervening to encourage progression to the next stage of learning. This lies within Vygotsky's theory that children have a zone of proximal development (see Figure 5.2) indicating their learning potential, with adult support. It should be remembered that practitioners, often feeling pressured by legislation and requirements, may feel inclined to direct or lead children's play, learning, progress and development too much by telling them what to do next or informing them how to overcome obstacles they are facing without giving them the time or opportunity to discover solutions for themselves. Perhaps more useful and practical learning will take place through a child's own process of trial and error and elimination. Identifying the problem and trying to discover ways around it can often produce more lasting knowledge and skills (Wall, 2006, p.105).

Key Term

Zone of proximal development: Vygotsky's description for a child's next area of development, where adult assistance is only required until the child has developed the skill and can do it independently.

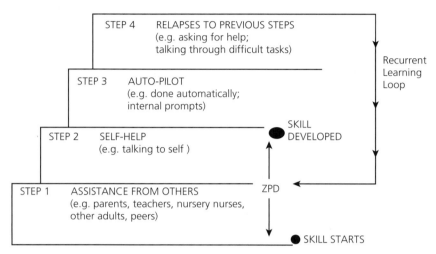

Figure 5.2 Vygotsky's 'zone of proximal development' (adapted from Tharp & Gallimore, 1991, p.50)

Practitioners can play alongside a child and then use the Playladders (see Chapter 4) approach to recording, or take notes throughout the period, which can be transcribed in more detail later if required. Alternately, an adult can observe a child playing with another adult and make detailed observations. Sometimes this approach has the benefit of enabling greater objectivity and can highlight issues surrounding the practitioner and his/her approach, as opposed to the child's development. Subsequent observational records can then be shared with parents and other practitioners at progress review meetings. In addition, discussions after the observation could highlight different adult interpretations of the same event (Wall, 2006, p.105).

Observing through play

Current thinking supports the view that learning through play, with appropriate support or scaffolding by adults (see Figure 5.3), is an ongoing process in which all young children participate. For example, the baby who places everything into his/her mouth as part of early discovery; or the child who struggles to build a bridge to pass trains under and, through a process of elimination combined with trial and error, learns about shape, size, balance and develops fine motor skills. As so much learning occurs through play experiences, it makes sense to find ways to record evidence through observing children at play (Wall, 2006, p.104).

Key Term

Scaffolding: adult assistance given to support the child's thinking and learning, as the child develops competence the adult decreases support until the child works independently.

Figure 5.3 Scaffolding: supporting children's learning and development (from Kamen, 2007, p.238)

 *Activity*

How do practitioners in your setting observe young children's play?

Observing very young children's play

Very young babies are dependent on the adults who care for them to provide a wide range of interesting multi-sensory experiences to support the healthy development of their maturing brains. Treasure baskets are an ideal way to provide these experiences. A treasure basket is a collection of interesting natural and reclaimed resources and household objects put together to give a baby a safe yet intriguing range of objects to explore. The collection of objects in the treasure basket offers a baby the opportunity to make choices about what to select, whether or not to pick up an object at all, when to do so and for how long (Thornton & Brunton, 2010b).

Treasure baskets can be used with an individual baby or with two to three babies sharing the same treasure basket collection. They should be seated close enough to the basket to be able to reach the contents easily and have clear space around them to discard objects removed from the basket. The adult should sit close by and observe closely, but not interfere. The adult can offer reassurance through gestures and body language, but this is a time to sit back and observe closely rather than trying to direct the activity that is taking place. By observing closely while a baby is exploring the objects in a treasure basket, the practitioner will be able to learn a great deal about his or her interests, skills and dispositions. You can use these observations to build up a picture of the baby as an individual. Share your observations with the baby's parents and use the knowledge you have gained to plan what to offer the baby next to engage his or her curiosity and extend his or her learning and development (Thornton & Brunton, 2010b).

Figure 5.4 Practitioner observing a baby exploring a treasure basket

 Activity

Describe how *you* use observation and assessment to plan provision to promote children's development in your setting. Include examples of any planning sheets you use.

Developing appropriate educational programmes that encompass the key issues for each area of learning and development

It is vital that *all* children have access to a stimulating environment that enables learning to take place in exciting and challenging ways. To develop into healthy, considerate and intelligent adults, all children require intellectual stimulation as well as physical care and emotional security.

As a practitioner you should consider the individual needs, interests and level of development of each child in your care. You should use this information to plan a challenging and enjoyable experience for each child in all of the areas of learning and development. When working with the youngest children you should focus strongly on the three prime areas (personal, social and emotional development; physical development; communication and language) that are the basis for successful learning in the other four specific areas (literacy; mathematics; understanding the world; expressive arts and design). The three prime areas reflect the key skills and capacities all children need to develop and learn effectively. As children grow in confidence and ability within the three prime areas, the balance will shift towards a more equal focus on all areas of learning (DfE, 2012, p.6).

Developing appropriate educational programmes should also take into account the three key characteristics of effective learning, i.e. playing and exploring, active learning and creating and thinking critically (see Chapter 8).

Planning in the early years is about meeting young children's needs so that they can play and learn happily in ways that will help them develop skills and knowledge across the prime and specific areas of learning in the EYFS. Planning is different from setting to setting because each setting is unique for all sorts of reasons. Some settings will plan certain things in a similar way, however – these might be events that are planned every year, such as a visit to a farm or regular visits from an orchestra who work with the children, helping them to find out about several instruments and to listen to and join in some music-making or drama. These events are part of the setting's long-term planning. Between long-term planning and the experiences that are planned for children on a daily and weekly basis are the medium-term plans that are made to ensure that certain areas of learning are addressed over 6 weeks or a half term – for example focusing on particular stories to help children to think about 'friendship'. These type of plans need to be in place so that all the necessary resources such as books and props can be gathered. All planning should be flexible, however, and used as a guide rather than followed slavishly. The most important planning that is done is the short-term daily/weekly planning that arises from discussions with the children and their parents and is based around their current interests (EYM, 2012).

The planning needs to be flexible enough to allow for young children's individual interests as well as unplanned, spontaneous opportunities to promote children's development and learning. For example, an unexpected snowfall can provide a wonderful opportunity to talk about snow and for children to share their delight and fascination with this type of weather. Or a child might bring in their collection of postcards and prompt an unplanned discussion about the collections of other children; this might be developed into a 'mini-topic' on collections if the children are really interested. It is important that children have this freedom of choice to help represent their experiences, feelings and ideas. Adults may still be involved in these activities, but in more subtle ways, such as encouraging children to make their own decisions and talking with children while they are engaged in these types of activities.

 Activity

How have you made use of an unplanned learning opportunity?

Delivering each area of learning and development through planned and purposeful play

Each area of learning and development must be implemented through planned and purposeful play. Play is essential for children's development, building their confidence as they learn to explore, to think about problems, and relate to others. Children learn by leading their own play, and by taking part in play that is guided by adults (DfE, 2012, p.6).

Play provides opportunities for young children to choose activities where they can interact with other children or adults, or sometimes play alone. During these activities children learn by first-hand experience – by actively 'doing'. Children experience play physically and emotionally. Young children need sufficient space, time and choice with a range of play activities both indoors and outdoors. Using their observations of individual children's current interests, developmental needs and play needs, practitioners should plan and prepare opportunities for child-initiated activities as well as adult-directed activities (see below).

Children need a combination of real and imaginary experiences to encourage learning and development. This is why play is such an important aspect of young children's thinking and learning. Young children need to handle objects and materials to understand basic concepts.

For example, water play can help young children to learn about volume and capacity in fun ways. Through active learning, children use play opportunities to encourage and extend the problem solving abilities that are essential to developing their intellectual processes. (See 'Active learning' in Chapter 8.)

Supporting personal, social and emotional development

Personal, social and emotional development involves helping children to: develop a positive sense of themselves and others; form positive relationships and develop respect for others; develop social skills and learn how to manage their feelings; understand appropriate behaviour in groups; and have confidence in their own abilities (DfE, 2012, p.5).

(For information see Chapter 9 'Develop positive relationships with children, young people and others involved in their care' in Meggitt *et al.*, 2011, pp.157–63; and Chapter 8 'Supportive approaches to behaviour management' in Smith *et al.*, 2012, pp.251–382.)

Ten ways to support young children's personal, social and emotional development

You can help to support young children's personal, social and emotional development by:

1. **Using praise and encouragement** to help the children focus on what they are good at. Treat every child in the setting as an individual. Each child has unique abilities and needs. Help the children to maximise their individual potential.

2. **Taking an interest in the children's efforts as well as achievements.** Remember the *way* children participate in activities is more important than the end results, e.g. sharing resources, helping others and contributing ideas. Encourage the children to measure any achievements by comparing these to their *own* efforts. Foster co-operation between children rather than competition.

3. **Giving the children opportunities to make decisions and choices.** Letting children and young people participate in decision-making, even in a small way, helps them to feel positive and important; it also prepares them for making appropriate judgements and sensible decisions later on in life.

4. **Promoting equal opportunities by providing positive images of children and adults** through: sharing books and stories about real-life situations showing children (and adults) that the children can identify with; providing opportunities for imaginative play that encourage the children to explore different roles in positive ways, e.g. dressing up clothes, cooking utensils, dolls and puppets.

5. **Being consistent about rules and discipline.** All children need consistency and a clearly structured framework for behaviour so that they know what is expected of them. Remember to label the behaviour not the children as this is less damaging to their emotional well-being, e.g. 'That was an unkind thing to say' rather than 'You are unkind'.

6. **Setting goals and boundaries** to encourage socially acceptable behaviour as appropriate to the children's ages and levels of development. Using appropriate praise and rewards can help.

7. **Encouraging the children's self-help skills.** Be patient and provide time for the child to do things independently, e.g. choosing play activities and selecting own materials; helping to tidy up; dressing independently during dressing up.

8. **Providing opportunities for the children to participate in social play**, e.g. encourage children to join in team games, sports and other co-operative activities.

9. **Using books, stories, puppets and play people** to help children understand ideas about fairness, jealousy and growing up, dealing with conflict situations.

10. **Encouraging the children to take turns**, e.g. sharing toys and other play equipment. Emphasise co-operation and sharing rather than competition.

Activity

- Plan, implement and evaluate a play activity that encourages or extends a child's personal, social and emotional development. Use the assessment from your observation of a child's social and emotional development (on page 164) as the basis for your planning.
- Encourage the child to use a variety of emotional abilities and social skills. For example: imaginative and/or creative skills to express feelings; ability to make choices or decisions; positive behaviour; independence (e.g. using self-help skills or making choices); effective communication skills, including their ability to express needs and/or feelings; sharing resources; understanding the needs and feelings of others.

Supporting physical development

Physical development involves providing opportunities for young children to be active and interactive; and to develop their co-ordination, control, and movement. Children must also be helped to understand the importance of physical activity, and to make healthy choices in relation to food (DfE, 2012, p.5).

(For information see Chapter 20 'Promote young children's physical activity and movement skills' in Meggitt *et al.*, 2011, pp.427–39.)

Figure 5.5 Young children playing outdoors

Ten ways to support young children's physical development

You can help to support young children's physical development by:

1. **Selecting play activities, tools and materials** that are appropriate to the ages and levels of development of the children.
2. **Providing play opportunities that encourage the children to explore and experiment** with their physical skills both indoors and outdoors, with and without play apparatus or other equipment.
3. **Maintaining the children's safety** by providing appropriate adult supervision and checking that any equipment used meets required safety standards and is positioned on an appropriate surface. Ensure the children know how to use any equipment correctly and safely.
4. **Providing play opportunities that allow the children to repeat actions** until they are confident and competent. Provide specific tools and activities to help the children practise their physical skills. Encourage children to persevere with tackling new skills that are particularly difficult by reassuring the children that everyone needs practice and patience to learn new skills.
5. **Using everyday routines** to develop the children's fine motor skills, e.g. getting dressed, dealing with fastenings and shoelaces, helping to prepare or serve food, washing up, and setting out/clearing away play activities. (Remember safety.)

6. **Providing play opportunities** to help the children practise fine motor skills, e.g. bricks, jigsaws, playdough, sand, construction kits, drawing.
7. **Helping the children to develop body awareness** through action songs such as 'Head, shoulders, knees and toes'.
8. **Encouraging and praising the children** as they become competent in each physical skill.
9. **Allowing the children to be as independent** as possible when developing their physical skills.
10. **Adapting activities and/or using specialist equipment** for children with special needs to enable their participation in physical activities as appropriate.

 Activity

- Plan, implement and evaluate an activity that encourages or extends a child's physical skills. Use the assessment information from your observation of a child's physical development (on page 164) as the basis for your planning.
- Include examples of physical skills such as gross motor skills, fine motor skills and/or co-ordination skills.

Supporting communication and language development

Communication and language development involve giving children opportunities to experience a language-rich environment; to develop their confidence and skills in expressing themselves; and to speak and listen in a range of situations (DfE, 2012, p.5).

(For information about communication and language development, see Chapter 16 'Support children's speech, language and communication' in Meggitt *et al.,* 2011, pp.326–57.)

Ten ways to support young children's communication and language development

You can help to support young children's communication and language development by:

1. **Talking to babies and children about anything and everything!**
2. **Showing the children what you are talking about,** e.g. use real objects/situations, pictures, books, and other visual or audio aids.
3. **Using straightforward sentences** with words appropriate to the children's level of understanding and development; avoid over-simplifying language and do *not* use 'baby talk' – children need to hear adult speech to learn language.
4. **Using repetition to introduce/reinforce new vocabulary and ideas.** Do *not* make the children repeat things back over and over; this is boring and frustrating.
5. **Copying the children's sounds/words**, including any extensions or corrections to positively reinforce and extend the children's vocabulary, sentence structures, etc. For example, if the child says 'ball', you could reply 'Yes, that is Tom's red ball'. Or if the child says 'moo!', you could reply 'Yes, the cow says "moo"!' **Never** tell children off for making language errors, it will only make them reluctant to communicate in the future. Making mistakes is part of the language learning process.

6. **Being lively!** Use your tone of voice and facial expressions to convey your interest in what is being communicated.
7. **Remembering turn-taking in language exchanges**. Ask questions to stimulate the children's responses and to encourage speech.
8. **Looking at the children when you are talking with them.** Remember to be at the children's level, e.g. sitting on a low chair or even on the floor; do *not* tower over them.
9. **Letting the children initiate conversations** and listening to what they have to say.
10. **Sharing a variety of age appropriate books, stories and rhymes** with babies and children.

 Activity

- Plan, implement and evaluate an activity that encourages or extends a child's language and communication skills. Use the assessment information from your observation of a child's language and communication skills (on page 164) as the basis for your planning.
- Include a variety of communication techniques such as: active listening (e.g. listening carefully and focusing on what the child has to say); leaving time for the child to respond/talk; careful phrasing of adult questions and responses.

Supporting literacy development

Literacy development involves encouraging children to link sounds and letters and to begin to read and write. Children must be given access to a wide range of reading materials (books, poems and other written materials) to ignite their interest (DfE, 2012, p.5).

All seven areas of the EYFS provide opportunities for the development of children's literacy skills. The skills used may vary according to the area of learning and development. For example, children may be involved in activities that encourage them to: describe, interpret, predict and hypothesise in mathematics or understanding the world; express opinions and discuss design ideas in expressive arts and design.

There is no set age at which children are magically ready to read and write, although most children learn to read and write between the ages of 4½ and 6 years old. The age at which a child learns to read and write depends on a number of factors: physical maturity and co-ordination skills; social and emotional development; language experiences, especially access to books; interest in stories and rhymes; concentration and memory skills; opportunities for play.

(For information about literacy development see Chapter 13 'Supporting numeracy and literacy development in children and/or young people' in Smith *et al.*, 2012, pp.415–55.)

Activity

- Observe a small group of young children involved in a story session. Focus on the children's responses (e.g. any verbal and/or non-verbal communication used by the children), how the children interact with others and how the adult communicates with the children during the story session.
- Compare the development of each child you observed with the expected development for a child of this age, looking at all aspects of the children's development but with particular emphasis on the focus area (i.e. literacy skills). Include references to support your comments. Suggest further activities to encourage or extend the children's literacy development, including any appropriate resources.

Figure 5.6 Young children enjoying a story session

Ten ways to support young children's literacy development

You can help to support young children's literacy development by:

1. **Providing plenty of opportunities for children to talk** – children who are effective communicators often transfer these skills to reading and writing. Provide plenty of opportunities for discussion, such as: circle time; story time; problem solving during activities; follow-up to activities, e.g. after television programmes or stories; co-operative group work; games and puzzles; talking about key features when on outings.

2. **Sharing books, stories, poems and rhymes to introduce children to different literary styles or genres**, including picture books, storybooks, 'big' books, novels, poetry books, information books, dictionaries, encyclopaedias and atlases. This also includes looking at other types of printed materials, e.g. newspapers, magazines, comics, signs. These will encourage children's listening skills and auditory discrimination and provide stimulus for discussion and literacy activities as well introducing or extending their vocabulary.

3. **Encouraging children to participate in appropriate opportunities for play**, especially activities that encourage language and communication, e.g. role/pretend play such as dressing up, home corner, shop play, creative activities.

4. **Using displays as a stimulus for discussions and to consolidate learning**, e.g. wall and interactive table top displays with interesting objects to talk about, look at and/or play with, as well as recorded sounds to listen to, including voices, music, songs, rhymes and musical instruments.

5. **Providing opportunities for children to follow and give instructions**, such as: introducing or extending knowledge on a specific skill; specifying tasks (verbal and/or written on a board); listening to step-by-step instructions; explaining worksheets, work cards or textbooks; verbal instructions during an activity to keep children on task or to provide extra support for individual children; delivering verbal/written messages, errands.

6. **Encouraging children to participate in games to develop auditory and visual discrimination**, such as sound lotto and 'guess the sound' using the sounds of everyday objects or musical instruments. Encourage children to participate in matching games and memory games to develop visual discrimination and memory skills, e.g. snap, matching pairs, jigsaws and games like 'I went shopping…'. Provide fun activities to develop letter recognition, such as: 'I spy…' using letter sounds; going on a 'letter hunt' (looking around the classroom for things beginning with a particular letter); hanging up an 'alphabet washing line'; singing alphabet songs and rhymes.

7. **Providing opportunities for the children to write for different purposes and for different audiences**, such as: writing about their own experiences as appropriate to their age and level of development, e.g. news and recording events; creating their own stories and poems as a means of expressing their feelings and ideas; using class or group topics as well as the children's own interests to stimulate their ideas for stories and poems; using storybooks as a starting point for the children's own creative writing. Provide children with opportunities to write in different styles, such as writing letters, writing reports, writing step-by-step instructions, designing posters, signs and notices. Encourage children to use independent spelling techniques, e.g. word banks, personal word books and dictionaries.

8. **Using alternative writing methods** to release younger children or those with co-ordination difficulties (such as dyspraxia) from their physical limitations with writing, e.g. allowing them to dictate their ideas while an adult acts as scribe or using a tape recorder or word processor.

9. **Considering the individual interests and abilities of children**, including valuing children's home experiences and cultural backgrounds, and being aware of possible developmental or psychological difficulties that may affect their speaking and listening skills by carefully observing children's development and learning. (See page 90, 'Children with particular requirements'.)

10. **Using ICT to encourage or extend children's literacy skills**, including television, CD-Roms and the internet as additional stimuli for discussions and ideas. ICT can also be used to introduce or reinforce information on topics and themes within the setting. Remember that ICT is not a substitute for other forms of communication such as conversation and children's play.

Ⓐ Activity

- Plan, implement and evaluate a story session to encourage young children's literacy skills. Use the assessment information from your observation of a small group of children during a story session (on page 102) as the basis for your planning.
- Include a follow-up activity to extend the children's literacy skills. For example: discussion about the story; rhymes and/or songs related to the story; simple sentences with drawings or paintings depicting each child's favourite part of the story; creating a group book retelling the story.

Supporting mathematics

Mathematics involves providing children with opportunities to develop and improve their skills in counting, understanding and using numbers, calculating simple addition and subtraction problems, and describing shapes, spaces and measures (DfE, 2012, p.5).

Learning numeracy skills is the central part of mathematics, but children are also taught about geometry (e.g. space and shapes) and the beginnings of algebra (e.g. number patterns). Children need to develop numeracy skills that involve confidence and competence with numbers and measures including: using and applying mathematics; counting and understanding number; knowing and using number facts; calculating; understanding shape; measuring; handling data.

(For information about supporting mathematics see Chapter 13 'Supporting numeracy and literacy development in children and/or young people' in Smith *et al.*, 2012, pp.415–55.)

 Activity

- Observe a small group of young children involved in a play activity that encourages the children's understanding of mathematics, e.g. number, weighing, measuring, volume or capacity.
- In your assessment include information on: the mathematical concept(s) observed; any other intellectual skills demonstrated by the children during the observation (e.g. concentration levels, memory skills, problem solving, imagination and creativity, language and communication skills). Suggest further play opportunities to extend the children's understanding of the specified concept(s).

Ten ways to support young children's development in mathematics

You can help to support young children's learning and development in mathematics by:

1. **Encouraging children to use and apply mathematics to tackle and solve everyday practical mathematical problems.** Examples include giving change in shop play and real shopping trips (addition and subtraction). Exploring volume and capacity during sand and water play by filling various containers to encourage understanding of full, empty, half-full, half-empty, nearly full, nearly empty, more/less than, the same amount, then introduce idea of standard measures, e.g. litre of juice, pint of milk. Using weighing and measuring activities, such as: shop play (using balance scales to compare toys and other items); real shopping (helping to weigh fruit and vegetables); sand play (heavy and light); cooking activities (weighing ingredients to show the importance of standard measures).
2. **Providing opportunities for children to use and apply mathematics in the setting and wider environment.** Orientation exercises, nature walks, geography and environmental studies can develop numeracy skills; educational visits can also contribute to mathematics across the curriculum, e.g. visits to science museums.
3. **Encouraging young children to explore numbers** through playing games like dominoes, 'chutes and ladders' and other simple board games; looking for shapes/sizes and making comparisons; price tags and quantities in shop play and real shopping trips; number songs and rhymes like 'One, two, three, four, five, Once I caught a fish alive...'.

4. **Supporting children engaged in counting, calculating and solving mathematical problems**, e.g. addition and subtraction, then multiplication and division. Supporting older children in employing standard methods to perform mental and written calculations, including addition, subtraction, multiplication and division using whole numbers, fractions, decimals and percentages.

5. **Prompting children to communicate their reasoning about problems and explaining their solutions** using objects, pictures, diagrams, numbers, symbols and relevant mathematical language, e.g. using letter symbols in algebra, setting up and using simple equations to solve problems.

6. **Supporting children's use of calculator functions to complete complex calculations** and understand the answers calculators give in relation to the initial mathematical problem.

7. **Encouraging children to compare, estimate and measure a range of everyday objects**, e.g. developing an understanding of length by comparing everyday objects/toys and using mathematical language such as tall/taller/tallest, short/shorter/shortest, long/longer/longest, same height, same length; measuring objects using appropriate units such as centimetres, metres, kilograms, litres.

8. **Helping children to tell the time**: o'clock, half past and quarter past the hour; with older pupils telling the time in hours and minutes and solving problems relating to time using a 12-hour or 24-hour clock.

9. **Encouraging children to explore shape and space** through activities such as: games involving shape recognition; handling and describing the various features of basic shapes (e.g. use correct names for basic 2D and 3D shapes; know how many sides, corners or right angles a shape has); physical activities involving whole turns, half-turns and quarter-turns or right angles as well as spatial awareness, through e.g. PE, movement, dance. Helping older children to learn more about shapes and co-ordinates, constructing shapes (geometry), and measurement including using a ruler, protractor and compass to create lines, angles and 2D or 3D shapes.

10. **Using information and communication technology (ICT) to encourage or extend children's knowledge, understanding and skills in mathematics**, e.g. playing shape recognition games; writing instructions to create and change shapes on a computer; providing opportunities for children to select, collect, organise and present appropriate data using lists, charts, graphs, diagrams, tables, surveys, questionnaires and CD-Roms.

A Activity

- Plan and implement a mathematics activity for a young child or group of young children. Use the assessment information from your observation of a small group of young children involved in a play activity that encourages children's understanding of mathematics (on page 165) as the basis for your planning.
- Review and evaluate the activity afterwards. Include information on the intellectual skills demonstrated by the child or children during the activity as well as the effectiveness of your planning and implementation.

Supporting understanding the world

Understanding the world involves guiding children to make sense of their physical world and their community through opportunities to explore, observe and find out about people, places, technology and the environment (DfE, 2012, p.5).

As part of understanding their world, children and/or young people are constantly thinking and learning, e.g. gathering new information and formulating new ideas about themselves, other people and the world around them. Babies and young children use their senses to: explore their environment; investigate and participate in new experiences; develop new skills and abilities; discover how things work in the world around them. Research shows that babies are born with a wide range of sensory skills and perceptual abilities that enable them to explore their environment through hearing, sight, touch, taste and smell.

(For information see Unit CP 18 'Supporting science and technology development in children and/or young people' available at **www.hoddereducation.co.uk/cache.**)

 Activity

- Observe a young child engaged in an activity that encourages sensory exploration.
- In your assessment focus on: which senses were used by the child; the child's responses, including any language used; the child's concentration level; the physical skills demonstrated by the child, e.g. hand–eye co-ordination, manual dexterity, mobility. Suggest how you could encourage or extend the child's development.

Figure 5.7 The young child's visual and auditory experiences are supplemented by tactile exploration of their environment

Ten ways to support young children's understanding of the world

You can help to support young children's understanding of the world by:

1. **Providing plenty of opportunities and materials to increase the children's curiosity,** e.g. treasure baskets, posters, pictures, books, games, toys and other play resources.
2. **Encourage children to be observant by pointing out details in the environment,** e.g. colours, shapes, smells and textures; interesting objects such as animals, birds and vehicles; talking about weather conditions; taking them on outings; gardening; keeping pets.
3. **Providing opportunities and materials for exploratory play,** e.g. exploring the properties of sand in sand play, e.g. that wet sand sticks together and can be moulded, while dry sand does not stick and can be poured. Water play with plain, bubbly, coloured, warm or cold water helps children learn about the properties of water, e.g. that it pours, splashes, runs, soaks. (For both sand and water play, provide small containers and buckets to fill and empty, as well as sieves and funnels.)
4. **Encouraging tactile exploration** through activities that involve exploratory play such as handling sand, water, clay, dough, wood and other modelling materials such as clean household junk (empty boxes, etc.) and manufactured materials, e.g. wooden and plastic construction kits, as well as making collages using different textures or playing games using a 'feely' box or bag.

5. **Providing opportunities for repetition as well as gradually more challenging activities** by encouraging children to play with materials, toys and games more than once; each time they play, they discover different things about these activities. However, do not push children too hard by providing activities that are obviously too complex; instead of extending children's abilities, this will only put them off due to the frustration of not being able to complete the activity.

6. **Encouraging auditory perception** through activities such as: singing rhymes and songs; clapping games; awareness of animal noises and environmental sounds; listening to songs, rhymes, music, stories and everyday sounds on CDs; sharing books and stories; playing sound lotto; identifying musical instruments; speaking and listening activities, e.g. phonics.

7. **Encouraging visual perception** through activities involving exploration of the environment, including outings to the park, a farm or a nature reserve; looking at books, pictures, displays and photographs; using magnification to highlight details, e.g. magnifying glasses, binoculars and telescopes; playing matching games; playing with jigsaws; observing details using mirrors; participating in activities requiring letter and/or number recognition, including simple board games.

8. **Encouraging use of taste and smell senses** through activities such as: cooking; finding out about different tastes – sweet, sour, bitter, salty; finding out about different smells – sweet and savoury, fruit and vegetables, flowers.

9. **Participating in children's play to extend their learning** by asking questions, providing answers and demonstrating possible ways to use equipment when the child is not sure what to do. For example, a child can become very frustrated when struggling to do a jigsaw, but make sure your help is wanted (and necessary); use verbal prompts where possible to encourage children to solve the problem themselves.

10. **Remembering safety at all times.** It is important to allow children the freedom to explore their environment and to experiment with the properties of different materials. However, make sure that these materials are suitable for young children, e.g. small objects that can pose a choking hazard or glass objects that could be broken causing cuts *must* be kept well out of the reach of young children.

 Key Terms

Auditory perception: the processing and interpretation of sound as meaningful information.

Visual perception: the ability to process and interpret information using the eyes.

 Activity

1. Plan an experience to encourage a young child's understanding of the world. You could use your suggestions from the observation (on page 165) as a starting point.
2. A suitable experience might be:
   - Providing an opportunity for exploratory play, e.g. sand/water play, model-making.
   - Providing a visual stimulus for a baby, such as a mobile or activity toy/centre.
   - Devising a musical activity or sound game to encourage auditory perception.
   - Designing a tactile activity such as a 'feely' box/bag or treasure basket.
   - Implementing a cooking or tasting session (remember safety, food allergies and dietary restrictions).
   - Organising an outing where the focus is on exploring the environment using the senses, e.g. a visit to the local park or nature centre/trail; going on a 'bug hunt'.
3. Review and evaluate the experience afterwards. Include suggestions for extending the child's learning and development in this area.

Supporting expressive arts and design

Expressive arts and design involves enabling children to explore and play with a wide range of media and materials, as well as providing opportunities and encouragement for sharing their thoughts, ideas and feelings through a variety of activities in art, music, movement, dance, role play, and design and technology (DfE, 2012, p.5).

When supporting the development of art, drama and music skills, you should provide children and/or young people with opportunities to: explore their environment and/or investigate new information/ideas; discover things for themselves through a wide variety of experiences; feel free to make mistakes in a safe and secure environment using 'trial and error'; develop autonomy through increased responsibility and working independently; encourage and extend their knowledge and skills with appropriate support from adults (and other children/young people); learn to make sense of new information within an appropriate curriculum framework, e.g. EYFS.

Young children need opportunities to develop their imagination and creativity through activities involving the expressive arts and design. For example:

- **Painting** with brushes, sponges, string; finger painting, bubble painting, butterfly or blob painting; printing (e.g. with potatoes, cotton reels) and pattern-making (e.g. with rollers, stamps).
- **Drawing** using a variety of tools (e.g. crayons, pencils), and paper that children can use when they feel the need to express themselves through this medium.
- **Model-making** using clean and safe 'junk' materials or commercial construction materials (e.g. Duplo, Lego, Stickle Bricks) to create their own designs.
- **Collage** using glue and interesting materials to create pictures involving different textures, colours and shapes; this gives children an enjoyable sensory experience.
- **Playdough** and other materials such as clay can be used creatively; they are tactile too. Encourage the children to help with making homemade playdough to extend the learning experience.
- **Cooking** is an experience similar to working with playdough or clay except that the end product is (usually) edible. Remember to include 'no cook' activities such as icing biscuits, making sandwiches or peppermint creams, where the children can create their own designs.
- **Making music** using a wide range of musical instruments (e.g. using percussion instruments to create their own combinations of different sounds as well as simple rhythmic patterns and tunes).
- **Creative writing** opportunities where children can demonstrate their imagination and creativity through stories and poems.

(For information about supporting learning and development in the expressive arts and design see Chapter 11 'Support children and/or young people's development of art, drama and music' in Smith *et al.*, 2012, pp.336–78.)

 Activity

- Observe a child engaged in an expressive arts and design activity (e.g. art, drama, music).
- In your assessment, comment on the child's: imaginative/creative skills; concentration level; memory skills; use of colour, shape and/or sound; fine motor skills (e.g. pencil or brush control). You might also consider the emotional value of the activity. Also comment on the level of adult support provided during the activity. Suggest ways to encourage and extend the development of the child's skills.

Figure 5.8 Children exploring and experimenting with materials

Ten ways to support young children's development in the expressive arts and design

You can help to support young children's development in the expressive arts and design by:

1. **Providing opportunities for creative activities such as painting and drawing:** provide lots of paper, crayons and pencils. Chunky crayons and thick stemmed pencils are best for young children. Provide variety in drawing and painting activities by offering different materials, tools and techniques, e.g. chalks, pastels, charcoal, felt tips; sponges, different sized brushes, rollers; different sized paper, shaped paper, different textures. Include opportunities to make collages using glue and interesting materials to create pictures involving different textures, colours and shapes, and provide an enjoyable sensory experience too.

2. **Providing opportunities for sand and water play**, including small containers and buckets to fill and empty, as well as sieves and funnels. Water play with plain, bubbly, coloured, warm and cold water helps children to learn about the properties of water, e.g. it pours, splashes, runs, soaks. Sand play provides opportunities for exploring the properties of sand, e.g. wet sand sticks together and can be moulded, while dry sand does not stick and can be poured. Use 'washed' or 'silver' sand (not builder's sand as this might contain cement).

3. **Providing opportunities for model making:** clay, playdough and Plasticine can be used creatively; they are tactile too. In addition, use commercial construction kits (e.g. Lego Explore, Mega Bloks, Stickle Bricks), wooden blocks or clean and safe 'junk' materials to enable children to create their own designs.

4. **Providing cooking activities:** cooking provides a similar experience to working with playdough or clay except that the end product is (usually) edible. Include 'no cook' activities such as icing biscuits, making sandwiches or peppermint creams. Remember to follow your setting's health and safety requirements.

5. **Providing opportunities for imaginative/role play** that encourage children to explore different roles in positive ways as well as encouraging language and communication, e.g. role/pretend play such as dressing up, home corner, shop play. Provide a variety of resources for children to engage in imaginary play, e.g. clean unwanted clothing for dressing up activities not just commercially produced outfits; commercially produced resources that are well-made, durable and safe for children's use, such as child-size domestic play equipment; dressing up clothes, cooking utensils, dolls and puppets that reflect different cultures; space for children's imaginary games that require little or no props.

6. **Providing activities that encourage children to express themselves and to develop self-confidence,** e.g. circle games such as 'The name game' where each child takes it in turn to say 'My name is … and I like to … because …' or 'Circle jump' where each child takes a turn at jumping into the circle, making an action that they feel expresses them and saying 'Hello, I'm …'; then the rest of the children copy the action and reply 'Hello, …' (repeating the child's name).

7. **Providing activities that help children to develop their music skills:** music provides an interesting and exciting way for children to be creative, e.g. making their own combinations of different sounds plus simple rhythmic patterns and tunes. Introduce children to rhyme by clapping out the beat of a rhyme, a song, a simple sentence or the syllables in each child's name. These skills will also help with the children's language and communication skills, especially their early reading skills.

8. **Providing opportunities for children to use percussion instruments**, especially with young children, as it is easy for them to make rhythmic and melodic sounds without the experience and expertise required for more complex instruments such as recorders, guitars and pianos. Provide a portable box or trolley with a range of percussion instruments, including drums, tambourines, castanets, wood blocks, shakers, bell sticks, Indian bells, triangles, xylophones and chime bars. To begin with, provide young children with opportunities to play along with their favourite songs and rhymes. Encourage the children to decide which instruments might be suitable for particular songs, e.g. triangles and bells for 'Twinkle, Twinkle Little Star'. Also provide opportunities for children to experiment freely with the musical instruments.

9. **Providing plenty of interesting experiences to provide stimuli for art, drama and music activities.** For example: books about famous artists, playwrights and composers; displaying copies of famous artwork; listening to CDs; watching concerts and plays, etc. on DVDs; visiting theatres, art galleries, concert halls and other suitable music venues; inviting theatre-in-education companies, local theatre and music groups to perform within the setting; inviting parents/grandparents to read or tell stories in community languages.

10. **Provide opportunities for children to experiment with using different styles** including art, storytelling, drama, music and dance from other cultures; creating their own art galleries and/or art portfolios; producing and performing plays; filming and reviewing their own drama activities; providing opportunities for children to produce and perform music as well as filming and reviewing their own musical activities.

 Activity

- Plan and implement an expressive arts and design activity for a young child. You could use your observation of a child engaged in an expressive arts and design activity (on page 166) as the basis for your planning.
- Review and evaluate the activity afterwards. Include information on the art, drama and/or music skills demonstrated by the child during the activity as well as the effectiveness of your planning and implementation.

Child-initiated activity and adult-led activity

Each area of learning and development must be implemented through a mix of child-initiated activity and adult-led activity. There is an ongoing judgement to be made by practitioners about the balance between activities led by children and activities led or guided by adults. Practitioners must respond to each child's emerging needs and interests, guiding their development through warm, positive interaction. As children grow older, and as their development allows, it is expected that the balance will gradually shift towards more activities led by adults, to help children prepare for more formal learning, ready for Year 1 (DfE, 2012, p.6).

Supporting child-initiated activity

Child-initiated activity has important benefits for young children's development. For example, it helps to promote their self-confidence and independence. It provides opportunities for young children to: try things out; solve problems; be creative; take risks; use trial and error to find things out. In their play young children use the experiences they have and extend them to build up ideas, concepts and skills. While playing young children can express their fears and re-live anxious experiences in a safe and secure environment. For example, role play allows children to take on and rehearse new and familiar roles.

You should aim to provide minimum intervention in child-initiated activity while keeping children safe from harm. For example, you will need to intervene when boisterous play becomes unsafe. You should support rather than direct child-initiated activity. You should help to create a play environment that will stimulate child-initiated activity and provide maximum opportunities for children to experience a wide variety of play types.

Five ways to support child-initiated activity

You can help to support child-initiated activity in the following ways:

1. **Use your observations of children's play to plan and create play spaces that meet their play needs and preferences.** Evaluate the play provision regularly to ensure it continues to meet children's changing play needs and preferences. Value the play of all the children, even those who tend to play noisily or base their play on themes with which you are unfamiliar, e.g. video game characters.
2. **Provide flexible resources that can be used in many different ways to facilitate children's play**, e.g. boxes, clothes horses, blankets and tablecloths to make dens and shelters. Set out resources and encourage children to select their own resources.
3. **Provide opportunities for all children to explore different materials and activities**, as well as offering alternative activities if appropriate. Provide new materials and tools to stimulate children's exploration and learning.
4. **Extend and develop children's language and communication in their play through sensitive observation and appropriate intervention.** Observe children's play and help children to join in if they find it hard to be included, but watch and listen carefully before intervening. Know when to get involved and when to allow children to carry on playing, e.g. joining in with children's play if and when invited. Intervene in children's play if it is racist, sexist or in any way offensive, unsafe, violent or bullying.
5. **Support children with disabilities/special educational needs**, e.g. by ensuring accessibility to resources, adapting the environment (such as the furniture layout) and maximising the use of space in the setting to allow freedom of movement for *all* children (including those who with physical disabilities or visual impairment).

Activity

- Observe a child or small group of children involved in a child-initiated activity. Make notes on what the child/children are doing and what the developmental benefits are.
- What opportunities for child-initiated activity are provided in your setting? Make a list of resources that might support child-initiated activity.
- Give examples of how an adult could support child-initiated activity. Identify the role of adults in providing for child-initiated activity. Explain why adults might intervene during child-initiated activity.

Planning adult-led activity

Adult-directed activities provide opportunities for children to experience sustained learning and shared thinking as well as developing specific skills such as literacy and numeracy. The role of the adult in supporting adult-directed activities include: encouraging children's language and thinking skills; monitoring children's interest; providing encouragement; preparing materials and providing resources; providing differentiation for children with SEN/disabilities; evaluating provision.

When planning adult-directed activities, practitioners should consider the following: the age of the children; the children's levels of development and their developmental needs; the children's interests; diversity, e.g. ensuring activities reflect the cultural diversity of the setting; inclusion, e.g. ensuring activities are accessible to children with disabilities/special needs; links to the relevant early years curriculum, e.g. EYFS.

You can write down your plans for an adult-led activity on a planning sheet or in an activity file. Your plans may be brief or detailed depending on the requirements of your setting. Some activities may require more detailed preparation and organisation than others, e.g. arts and crafts, cooking, outings. The senior practitioner, setting manager or your college tutor/assessor should give you guidelines on how to present your routine and activity plans. If not, you might find this suggested format useful:

Title: brief description of the activity
Date and time: the date and time of the activity
Planned duration: how long will the activity last?
Aim and rationale: the main purpose of the activity, including how it will encourage development, learning and/or behaviour. The rationale should outline why this particular activity has been selected (e.g. that you identified a particular child's need through observation; links to topics/themes within the group, class or setting). How does the activity link with the areas of learning and development in the EYFS?
Staff and setting: the roles and number of staff involved in the activity plus the type of setting and the age range of the setting.

Details of the child/children: activity plans involving an individual child or small group of children should specify first name, age in years and months plus any relevant special needs; activity plans involving larger groups should specify the age range and ability levels.
Learning objectives for the child/children: indicate what the child or children could gain from participating in the activity in each developmental area (**SPICE**).
Preparation: what do you need to prepare in advance? (For example, selecting or making appropriate materials; checking availability of equipment.) Think about the instructions and/or questions for the child or children; will these be spoken and/or written down, e.g. on a worksheet/card or on the board? Do you need prompt cards for instructions or questions?
Resources: what materials and equipment will you need? Where will you get them from? Are there any special requirements? Remember equal opportunities including special needs. How will you set out the necessary resources? (For example, setting out on the table ready, or the children getting materials and equipment out for themselves.)
Organisation: where will you implement the activity? How will you organise the activity? How will you give out any instructions the children need? Will you work with children one at a time or as a group? Are there any particular safety requirements? How will you organise any tidying up after the activity? Will the children be encouraged to help tidy up?
Implementation: describe what happened when you implemented the activity with the child or children. Include any alterations to the original plan, e.g. changes in timing or resources.
Equal opportunities: indicate any multicultural aspects to the activity and any additional considerations for children with special needs.
Review and evaluation: review and evaluate the following: • The aims and learning outcomes/objectives. • The effectiveness of your preparation, organisation and implementation. • What you learned about development and learning. • What you learned about planning activities. • Possible modifications for future similar activities.
References and/or bibliography: the review and evaluation may include references appropriate to development, learning and behaviour. Include a bibliography of any books used as references or for ideas when planning the activity.

Table 5.7 Planning sheet for an adult-led activity

All settings have a responsibility to provide a broad and balanced curriculum for all children. Settings use the EYFS as the starting point for planning play and learning activities that meet the specific developmental and learning needs of both each age group *and* individual children. You should work with colleagues to provide for the individual needs of each child in the setting, including differentiation for children with disabilities and special educational needs.

Five ways to support children's individual needs through adult-led activity

You can support young children's individual needs when planning adult-led activities by:

1. **Having high expectations and providing opportunities for all children to achieve success regardless of their race, gender or disability.** (This includes being aware of the requirements of the equal opportunities legislation relating to race, gender and disability.)

2. **Taking account of the different experiences, interests and strengths that influence the way children learn.** Securing children's motivation and concentration by planning work that builds on their interests and by varying subject content and presentation so that these match their learning needs. Setting appropriate targets for learning that build on children's knowledge, experiences, interests and strengths to improve areas of weakness and demonstrate progression over time.

3. **Taking account of the type and extent of the difficulty experienced by the child and providing curriculum access through greater differentiation of tasks and materials.** Using a flexible approach with children who have experienced gaps in their learning due to missed or interrupted education (e.g. travellers, refugees, children in care, children with long-term medical conditions, such as neurological problems, and children with degenerative conditions).

4. **Working closely, where appropriate, with specialists and representatives of other agencies who may be supporting the child.** Providing access to specialist aids and equipment or to alternative/adapted activities, following the advice and support of external specialists. For example: using visual/written materials and communication systems in different formats such as Braille or sign language; using ICT and technological aids; providing support from adults or peers when needed and adapting tasks or environments.

5. **Helping children to manage their emotions (particularly trauma or stress) and behaviour by creating a secure, supportive learning environment in which children feel safe and able to participate in a wide range of activities.** Providing positive encouragement and feedback that promotes children's development and learning as well as building confidence and positive self-esteem.

(A) Activity

- Plan an adult-directed activity for a child or small group of children. You could use your observation of a child or small group of children involved in a child-initiated activity (on page 112) as the starting point for your plan.
- Review and evaluate the activity afterwards. Comment on how the activity promoted the child or children's learning and development as well as the effectiveness of your planning and implementation.

CHAPTER 6

Assessing young children's progress

This chapter will help you to understand the importance of assessing young children's progress, including:

✱ The principles of demonstrating young children's progress
✱ Differences between formal and informal observations
✱ Assessing aspects of learning and development
✱ Identifying areas of development that would benefit from support.

Introduction

Assessment includes: observing the children as they play and learn; talking with children and finding out what they know, can do and how they feel; analysing and interpreting what you see and hear. When you know what the children can do and know, you can decide what they need next. You will be able to identify activities that allowed real growth and development of skills, and through analysis you will be able to identify the factors that contributed to this success – and use them again to inform future planning. Effective assessment supports children's learning, affects future planning and contributes to professional development (O'Brien, 2005).

As a practitioner you can use assessment to:

● amend your short-term planning
● inform your medium- and long-term plans
● adapt activities to suit the needs of individual children
● modify tasks to match children's known abilities
● provide children with positive and specific feedback as they work and play.

(O'Brien, 2005)

In the past the EYFS was assessment-driven. The revised 2012 EYFS is less so; the emphasis is much more on supporting young children's well-being, including catering for additional needs as well as individual needs. Assessment in the revised EYFS is not about comparisons between children. Practitioners use assessment to identify where the child is on their own individual learning journey and to input additional support for the child's development and learning as required. Assessment should be informed by ongoing targeted observations of each child as well as informal knowledge and discussion with parents.

The principles of demonstrating young children's progress

There are four principles for demonstrating progress during the EYFS. This involves assessing a broad range of information to illustrate children's progress over time and across all seven areas of learning and development.

> ## Four principles for demonstrating young children's progress during the EYFS
>
> 1. Children in the EYFS should not be tested to obtain data.
> 2. Children's progress must be identified and analysed through a range of appropriate evidence – mostly observation of child-initiated activity.
> 3. Understanding a range of information in order to draw conclusions about children's progress and the effectiveness of the early years provision.
> 4. Record keeping and information sharing according to the procedures of the setting.

Children in the EYFS should not be tested to obtain data

Effective approaches to assessment will generate information or data that can be used for a range of purposes. Children in the EYFS should not be tested to obtain data (EYU, 2008).

Young children are well known to be poor test-takers, perhaps because they are confused by being asked questions that they think the tester must already know the answers to! There is reason to suggest that the younger the child being evaluated, assessed or tested, the more errors are made. This principle shows that the younger the children, the greater the risk is of assigning false labels to them. Another principle may also be appropriate: the longer children live with a label (whether true or false), the more difficult it may become to discard it. All methods of assessment make errors: the errors made by formal tests are different from those made by informal or anecdotal records and documentation notes; the errors made by specific checklists of behavioural items are different from those made by holistic impressionistic assessments. Awareness of the potential errors of each evaluation or assessment strategy can help to minimise errors in interpretation. It is a good idea to strive for a balance between global/holistic evaluation and detailed specific assessments of young children (Katz, 1997, p.6).

Children's progress must be identified and analysed through a range of appropriate evidence

The majority of this evidence will be drawn from observation of child-initiated activity. Effective practitioners will be able to identify how individuals and groups of children in their setting have developed and progressed in their learning (EYU, 2008).

Assessment plays an important part in helping parents, carers and practitioners to recognise children's progress, understand their needs, and to plan activities and support. Ongoing assessment (also known as formative assessment) is an integral part of the learning and development process. It involves practitioners observing children to understand their level of achievement, interests and learning styles, and to then shape learning experiences for each child reflecting those observations. In their interactions with children, practitioners should respond to their own day-to-day observations about children's progress and observations that parents and carers share (DfE, 2012, p.10).

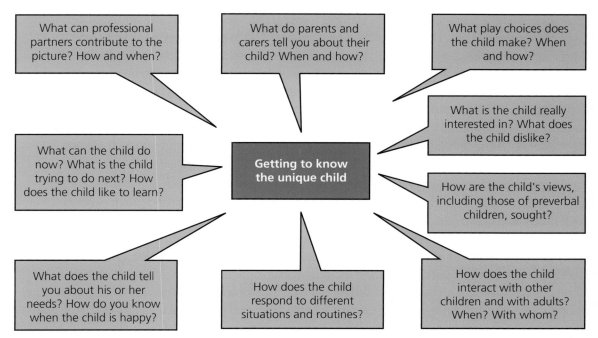

Figure 6.1 Getting to know the unique child (from DCSF, 2009, p.5)

Educators and child development specialists have long recognised the uniqueness of the early years. Informal assessment has characterised the early childhood field, e.g. early educators have observed and recorded children's behaviour naturalistically, watching children in their natural environments engaged in everyday activities. These observations have proven effective for purposes of chronicling children's development, cataloguing their accomplishments, and tailoring programs and activities within the classroom to meet young children's rapidly changing needs (Kagan *et al*., 1998, p.4).

Young children learn in ways and at rates different from older children and adults, so practitioners must tailor their assessments accordingly. Paper-and-pencil tests are not adequate because young children come to know things through doing as well as through listening, and they often represent their knowledge better by showing than by talking or writing. Tests may be very difficult or impossible to structure appropriately because young children do not have the experience to understand what the goals of formal testing are. Tests given at one point in time may not give a complete picture of learning because young children develop and learn so fast. Young children's achievements at any point are the result of a complex mix of their ability to learn and their past learning opportunities, so it is therefore a mistake to interpret measures of past learning as evidence of what could be learned. For these reasons, how we assess young children and the principles that frame such assessments need special attention. What works for older children or adults will not work for younger children; they have unique needs that we, as practitioners, are obliged to recognise if we are to optimise their development (Kagan *et al*., 1998, p.4).

Using portfolios as an assessment tool

Detailed individual observations of self-initiated activity in a particular context, photos and special moments contained in a child's portfolio all document the child's unique learning journey. Creating a portfolio is a useful assessment tool to support a young child with their understandings of concepts, ideas and emotional self. The final portfolio product could be used to provide evidence and to demonstrate accountability of meeting standards or benchmarks. A portfolio is a collection of items that celebrates the child. The portfolio includes a variety of artefacts, documentation and reflections that are developmentally appropriate for young children and includes evidence of understanding and ability. As an assessment tool, portfolios support and demonstrate children's understandings, abilities and talents through electronic, oral and hard copy formats. This collection may help guide curriculum and help learners become responsible for their own learning through the reflective process (Seitz & Bartholomew, 2008, p.63).

A high quality portfolio collection, with clear goals, is an intentional process of gathering items to help everyone involved in the assessment process (practitioners, children and parents) understand each child more completely and more in context. The complete portfolio and each individual component can be used as a formative or summative assessment depending on when and how often items are collected and evaluated, as well as the purpose. The portfolio process can help students become more self-directed and more responsible for their own learning. Remember that when planning portfolios, the child should be the focal point because the portfolio process provides opportunities to celebrate the child. However, practitioners and parents also play key roles as they help to guide the child through their learning. Throughout this process (the collection and sharing of work samples, reflections, observations and assessments) the child, practitioner and parent work together to celebrate the child's strengths and identify areas where the child needs to improve or continue to develop (Seitz & Bartholomew, 2008, p.64).

Practitioners should understand the expected curriculum and standards appropriate for the children as well as how to meet developmental needs. When this happens, portfolios provide the opportunity to show evidence of progress as measured against standards and whole child learning. Children have a variety of learning styles, many of which are non-traditional ways that do not clearly demonstrate achievement through paper-and-pencil methods. Portfolios allow for children to share their growth and learning in ways that express their individuality. They also allow for practitioners, children, parents and others to focus on the process and not just achievement. The types of portfolio may vary depending on the particular requirements of the setting (see Table 6.1). Each of the various forms has benefits as well as challenges (Seitz & Bartholomew, 2008, pp.65–6).

Type	Components	Materials	Benefits	Challenges
Notebooks	• Table of contents • Personal statement or self-assessment • Dividers for each aspect of learning and development • Reflections • Goals	• Binder and dividers • Paper/card • Plastic sleeves • Artefacts (work samples) • Photographs • Assessments	• A keepsake • Easy to add content • Content is adjustable • Easy to share with one or two others	• Hard copy may get lost • Hard to share with large group • Hard to compare data with other products • Takes time to create

Type	Components	Materials	Benefits	Challenges
e-portfolios	• Table of contents • Personal statement or self-assessment • Sections for each aspect of learning and development • Reflections • Goals	• Computer with current software • Electronic template software (PowerPoint, presentation software, etc.) • Digital photographs or video clips • Printer • Web pages • CD or DVD burner and player	• A keepsake • Easy to add content • Content is adjustable • Easy to share with others electronically • Easy to add more components • Easy to archive	• Must have technology equipment • Must have technology knowledge and ability • Takes time to create
Displays	• Overview of the project, behaviour, skill, experience • Photographs • Descriptions of the photographs • Work samples	• Bulletin board space, or • Panel (poster board or tri-fold) on which to place materials • Stapler, tape or adhesive • Paper (coloured, photo, etc.) • Ink to print photos and descriptions	• Visible to others • Large group or individual experiences are displayed • Reflects how student(s) have met standards	• Not as personal • Information may be lost when the bulletin board is removed • Takes time to create

Table 6.1 Different types of portfolios (adapted from Seitz & Bartholomew, 2008, p.67)

When beginning this process, a key to success is patience. The use of portfolios takes time to plan, organise and implement. What and how we assess affects what is taught and how it is taught. It is important to make sure that the assessment truly measures actual learning performance and ability within a relevant curriculum in order to provide a better understanding of children's achievement and to make meaningful use of the results. The portfolio process can be a very beneficial tool that has lasting and meaningful results for children, parents, practitioners and the setting (Seitz & Bartholomew, 2008, pp.66–7).

A *Activity*

Think about how your setting identifies and analyses children's progress. For example:
● What are the types of information gathered and the range of evidence used?
● How are portfolios used to assess young children's development and learning?

Understanding a range of information in order to draw conclusions about children's progress and the effectiveness of the early years provision

The complexity of young children's development requires practitioners and managers to be able to understand a range of information in order to draw conclusions about children's progress and the effectiveness of their provision (EYU, 2008).

Simply gathering information about each child's progress is not enough. It is *how* this information is used to support children's opportunities and experiences that makes a difference to their learning and development. Practitioners should reflect on what they know about the children and use this knowledge to:

● Plan to meet each child's needs, perhaps through adjusting styles of interaction, introducing new experiences, changing routines, or rearranging the environment.
● Plan to support learning through offering linked opportunities to practise and consolidate, following up on identified interests, or extending observed learning in a specific area.
● Share insights with parents, enabling them to work with the setting to support their children's learning.
● Share information with other settings the child may attend, so both can better meet the child's needs and support learning.

(DCSF, 2009, p.8)

An important aspect of gathering and using information is having a clear oversight of the progress made by children in a setting. For example, being able to step back from the detailed day-to-day focus on individual observation and assessment and undertake periodic, systematic reviews to see how well children are learning and developing across all areas of the EYFS (DCSF, 2009, p.10).

Just as knowing how to provide effective support for individual young children comes from observing and reflecting on what is noticed, so making judgements about the effectiveness of the early years provision depends on observing the group and the interactions between the individuals. Practices that suited one group of young children in the past may need adjustment as a new group of children develops their own social interactions and preferences. For a new group of young children, an early years setting may:

● Adjust resources, arrangement of space or routines.
● Identify and plan to provide specific support for areas of learning that are relevant to a particular group of children.
● Share information to support continuity with settings that share a number of children during the day or week, for example settings sharing a site.

(DCSF, 2009, p.8)

Activity

Think about how you draw conclusions about children's progress and the effectiveness of your setting's early years provision. For example, ask yourself these questions:

● Does the provision support young children's learning and development?
● Are the activities and experiences provided appropriate to the children's ages and levels of development?
● What additional opportunities could be provided to extend children's learning?

Record keeping and information sharing according to the procedures of the setting

In order to track children's progress, settings need a system for channelling the wealth of information gathered about individual children into a manageable summary. In order to capture progress information, a robust system is needed for identifying the stages children are at and showing the progress they make over time across all seven areas of learning and development. There is no prescribed format for this system but it should be grounded in the principles of the EYFS (see 'How observation and assessment in early years settings should be underpinned by the four guiding themes of the EYFS' in Chapter 1) and derived from observational assessment as described in the EYFS (see 'The principles of effective and purposeful child observation and assessment' in Chapter 2). (See Chapter 3 for more information about record keeping and information sharing, including details of the Data Protection Act 1998.)

Differences between formal and informal observations

Practitioners use both formal and informal assessment information to figure out what is working and to identify which children need additional help (Kagan *et al.*, 1998). Observation helps practitioners to take note of and assess children's learning and development. Observations can be **formal** (planned out in advance, with a clear aim) or **informal** (unplanned – where the practitioner notices, for example, a significant event or behaviour occurring, and takes note of it).

Ongoing formative assessment is at the heart of effective early years practice.

Practitioners can:

● Observe children as they act and interact in their play, everyday activities and planned activities, and learn from parents what the child does at home (observation).
● Consider the examples of development given under the heading 'Unique Child: observing what children can do' to help identify where the child may be in their own developmental pathway (assessment).
● Consider ways to support the child to strengthen and deepen their current learning and development, reflecting on guidance given under 'Positive Relationships' and 'Enabling Environments' (planning). These columns contain some examples of what practitioners might do to support learning. Practitioners will develop many other approaches in response to the children with whom they work.
● Where appropriate, use the development statements to identify possible areas in which to challenge and extend the child's current learning and development (planning).

(Early Education, 2012, p.3)

(Take another look at Figure 1.1 'Observation, assessment and planning to support each child's development and learning'.)

The support material Development Matters in the Early Years Foundation Stage (see Further reading) can help practitioners to support children's learning and development, by closely matching what they provide to a child's current needs. It states:

> 'Children develop at their own rates, and in their own ways. The development statements and their order should not be taken as necessary steps for individual children. They should not be used as checklists. The age/stage bands overlap because these are not fixed age boundaries but suggest a typical range of development.'

(Early Education, 2012)

Need for formal observations

Clarifying the main purpose for which young children are assessed can help determine what kinds of assessments would be most appropriate. Assessment of individual children might serve one of the following purposes:

- To determine progress on significant developmental achievements.
- To make placement or promotion decisions.
- To diagnose learning and teaching problems.
- To help in instruction and curriculum decisions.
- To serve as a basis for reporting to parents.
- To assist a child with assessing his or her own progress.

(Katz, 1997, p.6)

For the purposes of assessment, formal (planned) observations are often used. The EYFS requires early years practitioners to review children's progress and share a summary with parents at two points: in the prime areas between the ages of 24 and 36 months (see Chapter 7); and at the end of the EYFS in the EYFS Profile (see Chapter 8). Development Matters in the Early Years Foundation Stage (see Further reading) might be used by early years settings throughout the EYFS as a guide to making best-fit judgements about whether a child is showing typical development for their age, may be at risk of delay or is ahead for their age. Summative assessment supports information sharing with parents, colleagues and other settings (Early Education, 2012, p.3).

 Activity

Give examples of how your setting uses summative assessment to support information sharing with parents, colleagues and other settings.

Assessing aspects of learning and development

Assessments of young children should address the full range of early learning and development, including the three prime areas (personal, social and emotional development; physical development; communication and language) and the four specific areas (literacy; mathematics; understanding the world; expressive arts and design). Methods of assessment should recognise that children need familiar contexts in order to be able to demonstrate their abilities.

Practitioners do not need to collect physical evidence for everything for every child; after all children in the EYFS are *working towards* the Early Learning Goals (see Chapter 8). The prime areas are the most important part of the EYFS. Children must be secure in the prime areas before equal emphasis is given to the specific areas. The key focus of assessment should be on the prime areas. Practitioners should concentrate on tracking rather than documenting every detail of children's progress throughout the EYFS, including gathering *some* evidence for each area of learning and development.

Areas of learning and development	Aspects of learning and development
Prime areas:	
Personal, social and emotional development	● Making relationships ● Self-confidence and self-awareness ● Managing feelings and behaviours
Physical development	● Moving and handling ● Health and self-care
Communication and language	● Listening and attention ● Understanding ● Speaking
Specific areas:	
Literacy	● Reading ● Writing
Mathematics	● Numbers ● Shape, space and measure
Understanding the world	● People and communities ● The world ● Technology
Expressive arts and design	● Exploring and using media and materials ● Being imaginative

Table 6.2 Aspects of learning and development (Early Education, 2012, *Development Matters in the Early Years Foundation Stage (EYFS)*, p.6)

Aspects of personal, social and emotional development

Personal, social and emotional development involves helping children to develop a positive sense of themselves and others; to form positive relationships and develop respect for others; to develop social skills and learn how to manage their feelings; to understand appropriate behaviour in groups; and to have confidence in their own abilities (DfE, 2012, p.5).

Figure 6.2 Assessing young children's personal, social and emotional development

Observing aspects of children's personal, social and emotional development can be difficult because it is all too easy to become subjective. Our interpretations may be included in the assessment of observations, but they need to be based on accurate and objective information. Observing and assessing these aspects of development requires the recording of interactions between children and other people, which can sometimes be influenced by our own interpretations of the events and interactions observed. One way to ensure objectivity is to use a chart to record the children's social skills and any interactions observed (see Table 4.3). Further charts and graphs can be seen in Chapter 4, for example, pie chart (Figure 4.4) and bar graph (Figure 4.5). These allow you to record information more accurately. Observing emotional development can be especially problematic as we cannot *see* feelings. We can see the *expression* of feelings or *reactions* to people and situations that indicate the child's responses, such as joy, relief, physical hurt or distress. Looking at the social context and the particular event or situation being observed should make it clearer which emotional response is indicated. (See 'Supporting personal, social and emotional development' in Chapter 5.)

 Key Terms

Objective: only recording what we *actually* see and hear.

Subjective: recording our *interpretation* of what we see and hear.

Children's names				
Self-help skills	**Shafik**	**Sukhvinder**	**Ruth**	**Tom**
Goes to the toilet	c	c	c	c
Washes own hands	c	c	c	c

Self-help skills	Children's names			
	Shafik	Sukhvinder	Ruth	Tom
Dries own hands	c	c	c	c
Chooses own snack/meal	a	c	c	n
Uses fingers to eat food	c	n/a	n/a	c
Uses spoon	c	c	c	c
Uses fork	a	c	a	x
Uses knife	n	a	a	x
Holds cup with two hands	c	c	c	c
Holds cup with one hand	n	c	a	n

Table 6.3 Tick chart: group observation of children aged 4 to 5 years at lunchtime (c = competent at skill, a = attempts skill or needs adult direction, n = no attempt or requires adult assistance)

 Activity

- Use the information in Table 6.3 to assess young children's self-help skills.
- Refer to the developmental charts in Chapter 5 and any other relevant sources.
- Suggest ways to extend each child's development in this area.

Figure 6.3 Assessing young children's physical development

Aspects of physical development

Physical development involves providing opportunities for young children to be active and interactive; and to develop their co-ordination, control and movement. Children must also be helped to understand the importance of physical activity, and to make healthy choices in relation to food (DfE, 2012, p.5).

Young children need plenty of opportunities to develop their gross motor skills, fine motor skills and co-ordination through a wide choice of activities and experiences. They need both indoor and outdoor play areas, including cosy places with soft furnishings to have time out to be alone or with a friend, as well as spaces to build dens both indoors and outdoors. In addition children need to learn about keeping themselves healthy and safe including managing risk for themselves. (See 'Supporting physical development' in Chapter 5.)

Activity

- Use the information in Table 6.3 to assess young children's physical skills.
- Refer to the developmental charts in Chapter 5 and any other relevant sources.
- Suggest ways to extend each child's development in this area.

Aspects of communication and language

Communication and language development involves giving children opportunities to experience a rich language environment; to develop their confidence and skills in expressing themselves; and to speak and listen in a range of situations (DfE, 2012, p.5).

Figure 6.4 Assessing young children's communication and language development

Adults need to provide plenty of opportunities to encourage young children's language and to make appropriate responses to stimulate young children's communication. Remember that speaking is not just about words, it's also about articulating sounds, e.g. babies initiate 'conversations' and then adults respond. If adults do not respond, babies will stop initiating these conversations. Practitioners can encourage language development by providing a wide range of experiences and resources as well as encouraging children to talk about their interests, what they are doing and what is happening around them, and so on.

It can be difficult to be aware of your own communication skills in a busy early years setting. Recording your interactions with children is a helpful way to obtain information; you can then assess your questions/responses to the children, your tone of voice and speed of speech, as well as assessing the child's use of language and communication skills. Try recording language and communication in different situations, e.g. the role play area, book corner, outdoor space. There may be potential problems with recording children's activities, however, as it takes time to develop the technique; in addition the setting may be very busy and noisy, and individual children's skills may be difficult to identify. (See 'Supporting communication and language development' in Chapter 5.)

Activity

- Use the structured record sheet in Table 4.7 to observe and assess a young child's communication and language skills.
- Refer to the developmental charts in Chapter 5 and any other relevant sources.
- Suggest ways to extend each child's development in this area.

Aspects of literacy

Figure 6.5 Assessing young children's literacy development

Literacy means the ability to read and write. It makes sense to use the term 'literacy' as the skills of reading and writing complement one another and are developed together. Reading and writing are forms of communication based on spoken language. Children need effective speaking and listening skills in order to develop literacy skills. Literacy unites the important skills of reading, writing, speaking and listening.

Literacy development involves encouraging children to link sounds and letters and to begin to read and write. Children must be given access to a wide range of reading materials (books, poems, and other written materials) to ignite their interest (DfE, 2012, p.5).

Reading skills checklist

1. Can the child see and hear properly?
2. Are the child's co-ordination skills developing within the expected norm?
3. Can the child understand and follow simple verbal instructions?
4. Can the child co-operate with an adult and concentrate on an activity for short periods?
5. Does the child show interest in the details of pictures?
6. Does the child enjoy looking at books and joining in with rhymes and stories?
7. Can the child retell parts of a story in the right order?
8. Can the child tell a story using pictures?
9. Can the child remember letter sounds and recognise them at the beginning of words?
10. Does the child show pleasure or excitement when able to read words in school?

If the answer is 'yes' to most of these questions, the child is probably ready to read; if the answer is 'no' to any of the questions, the child may need additional support or experiences in those areas before they are ready to read.

Reading approaches

Whole word or 'look and say' approach

Children are taught to recognise a small set of key words (usually related to a reading scheme) by means of individual words printed on flashcards. Children recognise the different words by shape and other visual differences. Once children have developed a satisfactory sight vocabulary, they go on to the actual reading scheme. The whole word approach is useful for learning difficult words that do not follow the usual rules of English language. The drawback is that this approach does not help children to work out new words for themselves.

Phonics approach

With this approach children learn the sounds that letters usually make. This approach helps children establish a much larger reading vocabulary fairly quickly as they can 'sound out' new words for themselves. The disadvantage is that there are many irregular words in the English language; one letter may make many different sounds, e.g. b**ou**gh, r**ou**gh, thr**ou**gh. Children do better with the phonics approach than any other approach, however.

Apprenticeship approach

This approach, also known as the 'story' or 'real books' approach, does not formally teach children to read. Instead the child sits with an adult and listens to the adult read; the pupil starts reading along with the adult until the child can read some or the entire book alone. This approach does not help child with the process of decoding symbols. There has been much criticism of this approach, but it has proved effective in this country and New Zealand as part of the Reading Recovery programme for older less able readers.

Most practitioners helping children to develop reading skills use a combination of the 'look and say' approach to introduce early sight vocabulary and then move on to the more intensive phonics approach to establish the children's reading vocabulary. It is important for you to be flexible to meet the individual literacy needs of children; you should also work with parents to develop their children's reading skills.

Most activities used to develop children's early reading skills will also help children's early writing skills. In addition, young children need plenty of opportunities to develop the co-ordination skills necessary for writing (hand–eye co-ordination, fine motor skills for pencil control, being able to sit still with the correct posture). It is usual to teach writing skills alongside reading. This helps the children to make the connection between the written letters and the sounds they make when read.

Provide lots of opportunities for young children to develop the co-ordination skills needed for writing. Include activities such as: drawing and painting; colouring in; tracing; threading beads; cutting and sticking; sewing and weaving. Learning to write takes lots of practice so provide plenty of opportunities for young children to form letters in a variety of ways, for example: in the air; in sand; using paints; with crayons, pencils, felt tips; using Plasticine, clay or playdough.

Remember that some children may have special needs that require reading and/or writing using alternative means or specialist equipment such as Braille, word processing, or voice-activated computer. (See 'Supporting literacy development' in Chapter 5.)

 Activity

1. Observe a young child engaged in a writing activity. In your assessment comment on:
   - The child's fine motor skills and hand–eye co-ordination.
   - The children's concentration during the activity.
   - The creativity of the finished piece of writing.
2. Suggest ways to encourage and extend the child's writing skills.

Aspects of mathematics

Supporting mathematics involves providing children with opportunities to develop and improve their skills in counting, understanding and using numbers, calculating simple addition and subtraction problems, and describing shapes, spaces and measures (DfE, 2012, p.5).

Mathematics relies on the ability to understand abstract ideas. For young children this means developing a sound knowledge and understanding of concrete concepts first, such as number, weights, measures, volume and capacity. Experiences with real objects enable young children to develop problem solving skills and to acquire understanding of these concepts. Some concepts require the understanding of other concepts beforehand, e.g. understanding *number* and *counting* comes before *addition*; understanding *addition* comes before *multiplication*, etc. Practitioners need to ensure that they provide activities at the appropriate level for the children's conceptual development. There should be a balance between encouraging the children to develop their own problem solving skills through play with minimal adult intervention and complying with the learning and development requirements for mathematics in the EYFS. (See 'Supporting mathematics' in Chapter 5.)

Figure 6.6 Assessing young children's development in mathematics

A Activity

1. Observe a child engaged in an activity that encourages the child's development in mathematics, e.g. singing number songs and rhymes; sorting shapes, measuring or shopping; playing number games. In your assessment, comment on:
   - The mathematical skills demonstrated by the child.
   - The child's communication skills, including any mathematical language used.
2. Suggest ways to encourage and extend the child's or children's understanding of mathematics.

Aspects of understanding the world

Understanding the world involves guiding children to make sense of their physical world and their community through opportunities to explore, observe and find out about people, places, technology and the environment (DfE, 2012, p.5).

Understanding the world (or science) also relies on the ability to understand abstract ideas. For young children this means developing a sound knowledge and understanding of concrete concepts first, such as shape, colour, space, texture, growth and physical forces.

Figure 6.7 Assessing young children's development in understanding the world

Experiences with real objects enable young children to develop problem solving skills and to acquire understanding of these concepts. Young children need lots of opportunities to develop the following scientific skills: observe; investigate; predict; hypothesise; record. There should be a balance between encouraging the children to develop their own problem solving skills through play with minimal adult intervention and complying with the learning and development requirements for understanding the world in the EYFS. (See 'Supporting understanding the world' in Chapter 5.)

Activity

1. Observe a child engaged in an activity that encourages the child's development in understanding the world, e.g. sand and/or water play, cooking session, exploring colour or patterns, investigating the environment or weather conditions. In your assessment, comment on:
   - The scientific skills that were demonstrated by the child.
   - How the child was encouraged to explore using their senses.
2. Suggest ways to encourage and extend the child's or children's understanding of the world.

Aspects of expressive arts and design

Expressive arts and design involves enabling children to explore and play with a wide range of media and materials, as well as providing opportunities and encouragement for sharing their thoughts, ideas and feelings through a variety of activities in art, music, movement, dance, role play, and design and technology (DfE, 2012, p.5).

Figure 6.8 Assessing young children's development in the expressive arts and design

(For more information see 'Supporting expressive arts and design' in Chapter 5.)

 Activity

1. Observe a child or group of children engaged in an activity that encourages young children's development in the expressive arts and design. In your assessment, comment on:
   - The learning and development demonstrated by the child or children.
   - How the activity encourages the child or children to express themselves freely in an imaginative and creative way.
2. Suggest ways to encourage and extend the child's or children's learning and development in this area.

Identifying areas of development that would benefit from support

Throughout the early years, if a child's progress in any prime area gives cause for concern, practitioners must discuss this with the child's parents and/or carers and agree how to support the child. Practitioners must consider whether a child may have a special educational need or disability that requires specialist support. They should link with, and help families to access, relevant services from other agencies as appropriate (DfE, 2012, p.6).

Each child must be assigned a key person (a safeguarding and welfare requirement). Providers must inform parents and/or carers of the name of the key person, and explain their role, when a child starts attending a setting. The key person must help ensure that every child's learning and care is tailored to meet their individual needs. The key person must seek to engage and support parents and/or carers in guiding their child's development at home. They should also help families engage with more specialist support if appropriate (DfE, 2012, p.6).

(There is more detailed information about this in the section 'Identifying areas for concern' in Chapter 7.)

A *Activity*

- Look back over the observations you have undertaken during this chapter.
- Have you identified any areas of development that would benefit from support?

Finally, as practitioners, we need to be clear on: what we are assessing, why and how. We must ensure that the means used are appropriate and fair in order to avoid the crude labelling of individual children, which may result in a crushing experience for the child and be detrimental to future learning potential and motivation.

CHAPTER 7

Summary of development at age 24 to 36 months

This chapter provides you with information about the summary of development at age 24 to 36 months, including:

* **The purpose of the summary of development at age 24 to 36 months**
* **The content of the summary**
* **Identifying areas for concern**
* **Helping parents to support learning at home.**

Introduction

The Early Years Foundation Stage (EYFS) requires that parents and carers must be supplied with a short written summary of their child's development in the three prime learning and development areas of the EYFS (personal, social and emotional development; physical development; and communication and language) when the child is aged between 24 and 36 months (NCB, 2012, p.2).

This progress check must identify the child's strengths, and any areas where the child's progress is less than expected. If there are significant emerging concerns, or an identified special educational need or disability, practitioners should develop a targeted plan to support the child's future learning and development involving other professionals, e.g. the setting's Special Educational Needs Co-ordinator (SENCO) as appropriate (DfE, 2012, p.10).

 Key Term

Special educational need: all children have *individual* needs, but some children may have *additional* needs due to physical disability, sensory impairment, communication or social interaction difficulties, learning difficulties or emotional/behavioural difficulties.

The EYFS requires that providers carry out a progress check when a child is aged 2 years. The following factors may determine the timing of the progress check:

* **The child's entry point to the setting:** Settings should consider a settling in period for a child to enable their key person and other practitioners to build up good knowledge of that child's development, abilities and interests before completing the progress check.
* **Individual needs and circumstances:** If a child has a period of ill health or a significant event in their family (e.g. family breakdown, bereavement or the arrival of a sibling), it may be appropriate to delay the check.

based on a best-fit model, referring to the statements in Development Matters in the Early Years Foundation Stage (see Further reading). The child's particular interests are noted and next steps for learning are identified. The assessments are based on the practitioner's knowledge of the child, in partnership with parents, and parents are invited and encouraged to contribute their observations and thoughts (NCB, 2012, p.23). More examples of individual summaries are available from the NCB 'Know How' guide on pages 24–5 and 30–1 (see Further reading).

Reflecting the development level and needs of each individual child

For any assessment of development to be meaningful and useful, a complete picture of a child should be obtained. This will best be realised when parents, the child, and all practitioners and professionals who know or have involvement with the child, participate fully in the assessment process. A starting point for all assessment should be an acknowledgement that parents know their children best. They are their child's first and most enduring educators, with in-depth knowledge of their child's physical, emotional and language development over time. This knowledge should be reflected in both ongoing dialogue and in the progress check. The EYFS places a strong emphasis on working with parents as partners; this ongoing dialogue or sharing of regular two-way observations on learning and development with parents leads to improved cognitive, social and emotional outcomes for children. Parents and practitioners should reflect together on what:

- a child likes to do
- he/she is trying to master or has just learned
- new words/language structures are emerging
- particular interests or patterns in play and exploration are observed at the moment.

(NCB, 2012, p.8)

All children have a right to be listened to and valued in the setting. Children enjoy and can become very able at thinking about and assessing their own learning and development if this is recognised and supported well. They can help to record their progress, and identify what they have enjoyed or found difficult. Very young children and those with speech or other developmental delay or disability may not say anything or very little verbally, but they will communicate a great deal in other ways. This might be through gesture, action, body language or signing (NCB, 2012, p.7).

Early years professionals know and understand that young children are skilful and competent communicators from birth, communicating their views and experiences all the time, through the sounds that they make, their movement and actions. The key role of the adult is to listen, tune in to, document and reflect on this communication (Bryson, 2007).

 Activity

Find out about resources to support practice in listening to young children. You could start by looking at the 'Listening to young children' series of leaflets, which are available at: http://www.ncb.org.uk/ycvn/resources/practice-guidance

Highlighting observations about a child's development

Practitioners using the A Unique Child format (see Figure 7.3) make assessments based on knowledge gathered from observing the child over time and across a range of contexts. Discussions with parents feed into the summary, which is completed by the key person. In the section headed 'Your Child's Learning', brief comments are recorded reflecting the child's individuality in how they approach their learning – particular interests that arouse their curiosity, preferred ways of learning, and so on. The areas of learning and development are completed using Development Matters in the Early Years Foundation Stage (see Further reading) as a prompt to make best-fit judgements of the age band that best describes the child's current development and the band where the child is mainly working is highlighted. The key person also records a few comments that reflect the child's individuality in each area of learning. The 'Next Steps' section is used to record suggestions for supporting and extending the child's learning and development, both in the setting and at home. Consistency of judgements is achieved through staff discussing samples together, and setting leaders holding responsibility for ensuring consistent and reliable summaries are made. This has been adapted for the new EYFS requirements (NCB, 2012, p.27).

Noting areas where a child is progressing well

Practitioners provide regular written summaries of development for parents using All About Me. These are added to the child's ongoing record file (with photographs, records of children's creations, short notes and observations). The summaries and next steps are discussed with parents and their views and comments are included. The key person and parents plan opportunities and experiences to match a child's needs and interests together – and ideas are included in the 'At home I could' box (NCB, 2012, p.29).

The component cards in Birth to Three Matters (see Further reading) use the heading 'Look, listen and note' rather than 'observation' because '…what practitioners "notice" about babies and toddlers is often much more detailed and exciting than what actually gets recorded as an observation record' (Elfer, 2005, p.118).

'Look, listen and note'

What you 'notice' about what a child is able to do should form part of the record of the child's developmental progress. Suggested methods for observing the under-threes:

1. Observe for 10–20 minutes, focusing on one child and their interactions with adult(s) and other children and toys and objects.
2. Observe without a notebook, concentrating as much as possible on the chosen child, and being as receptive as possible to the smallest of details as well as emotional atmospheres and responses.
3. After the observation, make a written record of what you observed, writing in as free-flowing a way as possible, following the main sequence of events and recording details as they come to mind.
4. Share and discuss the written observation with your supervisor/colleagues; consider and examine differing interpretations and connections.
5. Continue further observations and bring your write-ups to the group to be discussed and compared.

(Miller, 2002)

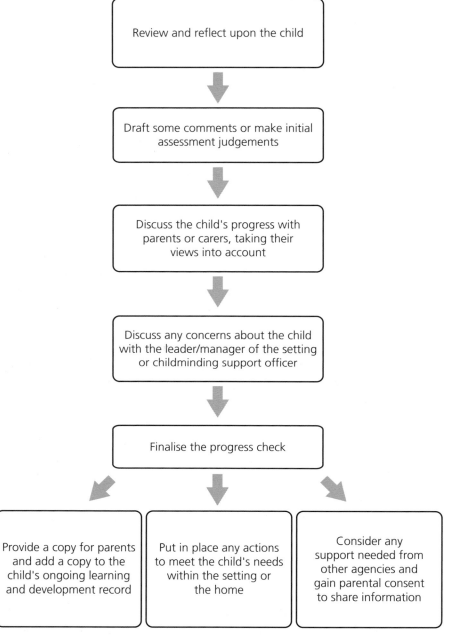

Review and reflect upon the child

Draft some comments or make initial assessment judgements

Discuss the child's progress with parents or carers, taking their views into account

Discuss any concerns about the child with the leader/manager of the setting or childminding support officer

Finalise the progress check

Provide a copy for parents and add a copy to the child's ongoing learning and development record

Put in place any actions to meet the child's needs within the setting or the home

Consider any support needed from other agencies and gain parental consent to share information

Figure 7.4 Suggested process for practitioners completing the progress check (NCB, 2012, p.13)

Observations and assessments (whatever methods you use in your setting) should not only be used to record developmental progress but also to inform practice, e.g. planning for young children's future developmental needs (see Chapter 5).

Activity

Outline how you observe, assess and record the developmental progress of babies and children under 3 years. Include information on:

- The relevant framework applicable to children in your setting.
- Your setting's policies and procedures for observing and assessing children's development, including agreed formats for observation and assessment.
- Sharing information about children's development with their parents, colleagues and other professionals in line with the setting's policies and procedures and any legal requirements, e.g. confidentiality and data protection.

Noting where there are concerns about the child's development or learning

Throughout the early years, if a child's progress in any prime area gives cause for concern, practitioners must discuss this with the child's parents and/or carers and agree how to support the child. Practitioners must consider whether a child may have a special educational need or disability that requires specialist support. They should link with, and help families to access, relevant services from other agencies as appropriate (DfE, 2012, p.6).

Supporting young children with special educational needs (SEN) and/or disabilities involves establishing the strengths and needs of children in partnership with their families and in collaboration with other agencies. It also involves the identification and provision of appropriate resources to enable inclusion and participation.

You must know, understand and follow the relevant legislation regarding children with disabilities and SEN. This includes supporting the setting in carrying out its duties towards pupils with SEN and ensuring that parents are notified of any decision that SEN provision is to be made for their child. (See Chapter 21 'Supporting disabled children and young people and those with specific requirements' in Meggitt *et al.*, 2011.)

Additional support for children with SEN in early education settings may be provided through Early Years Action, Early Years Action Plus and statutory assessment.

Early Years Action

Young children identified as having SEN may require support in addition to the usual provision of the setting. The SENCO, in consultation with practitioners and the child's parents will decide what additional support is needed to help the child to make progress. Additional support at Early Years Action may include: the provision of different learning materials or specialist equipment; some individual or group support provided by support staff (e.g. early years practitioners or teaching assistants); devising and implementing an individual education plan (see Figure 7.5).

Early Years Action Plus

Young children with SEN may require additional support that involves external support services. The SENCO, in consultation with colleagues, the child's parents and other professionals, will decide what additional support is needed to help the child to make progress. Additional support at Early

Years Action Plus may include: the provision of specialist strategies or materials; some individual or group support provided by specialist support staff (e.g. early years practitioners or teaching assistants with additional training in SEN); some individual support provided by other professionals, e.g. physiotherapist, speech and language therapist; access to local authority support services for regular advice on strategies or equipment, e.g. educational psychologist, autism outreach worker; devising and implementing an individual education plan (see Figure 7.5).

Statutory assessment

A few young children with SEN in the setting may still make insufficient progress through the additional support provided by Early Years Action Plus. When a child demonstrates significant cause for concern, the SENCO, in consultation with practitioners, the child's parents and other professionals already involved in the child's support, should consider whether to request a statutory assessment by the local authority (LA). The LA may decide that the nature of the provision necessary to meet the child's special educational needs requires the LA to determine the child's special education provision through a **statement of special educational need**.

A statement of SEN is set out in six parts:

- **Part one:** general information about the child and a list of the advice the authority received as part of the assessment.
- **Part two:** the description of the child's needs following the assessment.
- **Part three:** describes all the special help to be given for the child's needs.
- **Part four:** the type and name of the setting the child should go to and how any arrangements will be made out of school hours or off school premises.
- **Part five:** describes any non-educational needs the child has.
- **Part six:** describes how the child will get help to meet any non-educational needs.

 Activity

Have a look at the section 'Preparing the progress check for a child with identified SEN or disabilities' on page 20 of the Know How Guide.

A targeted plan to support the child's future learning and development in the setting

Planning and implementing activities to enhance very young children's development should be based on your observations of each child (see above), your relationship with each child and your understanding of holistic learning. Effective planning for very young children involves: viewing children as powerful and competent learners; using your knowledge of children as active learners (see Chapter 8) to inform your planning; observing children closely and respecting them as individuals in order to plan rich, meaningful experiences; recognising that an experience must be holistic to be meaningful and potentially rich in learning; planning a rich learning experience around the whole child not around a specific area or component; taking a holistic approach to the planning process by recognising and building on the child's needs, skills, interests and earlier experiences; making your planning flexible and flow with the child (Abbott & Langston, 2005).

Individual Education Plans

All settings should differentiate their approaches to supporting learning and development to meet the needs of individual children. The strategies used to support the learning and development of individual children with SEN should be set out in Individual Education Plans (IEPs), whether they receive additional support in the setting as part of Early Years Action, Early Years Action Plus or statement of special educational need.

INDIVIDUAL EDUCATION PLAN (IEP): GENERAL GUIDANCE

<table>
<tr><td colspan="2">Name:</td><td>Date of Birth:</td><td>Age:</td><td colspan="2">Staff Involved:</td><td colspan="2">SENCO:</td></tr>
<tr><td colspan="2">IEP Start Date:</td><td colspan="2">Review Date:</td><td colspan="2">Signed:</td><td colspan="2">Signed:</td></tr>
<tr><td colspan="4">Strengths:
➢ Positive attributes to activities
➢ Preferred learning style
➢ Interests</td><td colspan="4">Areas to be developed (each area should have a corresponding target):
➢ Area/s to be prioritised
➢ The aspect of the prioritised area/s to be targeted</td></tr>
<tr><th>Targets</th><th colspan="2">Strategies</th><th colspan="2">Provision</th><th colspan="2">Success Criteria</th><th>Achieved</th></tr>
<tr><td>➢ To be addressed in an appropriate specified time</td><td colspan="2">➢ Any specific approach/ method/ programme to be used</td><td colspan="2">➢ Is extra adult support needed?
If so, who is to be involved in the delivery?</td><td colspan="2">➢ Monitoring and assessment arrangements
➢ How the targets can be evaluated</td><td>Date or notes to inform future action</td></tr>
<tr><td>➢ Specific
➢ Measurable
➢ Achievable
➢ Realistic
➢ Time related
➢ (Easily negotiated)</td><td colspan="2">➢ How the work may need to be differentiated to meet the individual need
- by the way it is presented
- equipment/materials used
- 'additional to and different from...'</td><td colspan="2">➢ Additional materials/ equipment necessary</td><td colspan="2">➢ How achievement can be measured</td><td></td></tr>
<tr><td>➢ Usually begins with:
- 'To know'
- 'To be able'
- 'To produce'</td><td colspan="2"></td><td colspan="2">➢ When and where the support will take place, e.g. in class during group time
➢ The time allocated for the session, e.g. 20 mins.</td><td colspan="2">➢ Usually ends with:
- 'By ... (date) ... (name) will achieve... ' e.g.
- 4/5 times
- with 80% success
- on 5 consecutive occasions</td><td></td></tr>
<tr><td colspan="3">Parent/Carer Involvement:
➢ Home/school link arrangements
➢ Strategies/activities for home</td><td colspan="2">Child's View:
➢ The view shown/expressed by the pupil</td><td colspan="3">Additional Information:
➢ Other agencies involved , e.g. EP, SALT, etc.
➢ Relevant medical information</td></tr>
<tr><td colspan="8">Evaluation and Future Action:
What progress/concerns/issues have arisen. The next steps to be made. Further contacts/advice needed.</td></tr>
</table>

Figure 7.5 Example of an early years Individual Education Plan (from: http://www.shropshire.gov.uk/ inclusion.nsf/open/5F1F3F90DE92EE8D80256CD2004B41FA)

A child's IEP should identify three or four individual targets in specific key areas, for example: personal, social and emotional development; communication and language; physical development. When supporting the development of IEPs remember to have high expectations of children and a commitment to raising their achievement based on a realistic appraisal of children's abilities and what they can achieve. You may be involved in regular reviews at least three times a year of IEPs in consultation with the SENCO, the child and their parents.

A child's Individual Education Plan should include the following information:

- The child's strengths.
- Priority concerns.
- Any external agencies involved.
- Background information, including assessment details and/or medical needs.
- Parental involvement/child participation.
- The short-term targets for the child.
- The provision to be put in place, e.g. resources, strategies, staff, allocated support time.
- When the plan is to be reviewed.
- The outcome of any action taken.

Documentation and information about the *Special Educational Needs Code of Practice*, including Early Years Action, Early Years Action Plus and statutory assessment should be available from your setting or the SENCO.

 Activity

Outline your setting's procedures for ensuring that Individual Education Plans for children are in place and regularly reviewed. Provide examples of the relevant forms, e.g. an Individual Education Plan; review sheets for child comments, parent comments and staff comments; record of review. Remember confidentiality.

Identifying areas for concern

Some young children may have been identified as having SEN prior to starting at the early years setting, e.g. children with physical disabilities, sensory impairment or autism. Other young children may not be making sufficient progress towards the Early Learning Goals or may have difficulties that require additional support within the setting.

The importance of early identification of special educational needs

The early identification of special educational needs (especially more complex needs) is important, as the earlier children receive tailored support to catch up, the stronger their subsequent chances of healthy development will be.

Early identification of SEN is very important and effective as early intervention to support young children's difficulties can prevent more complex problems later on. For example, the early identification of communication difficulties is important because:

1. Language and communication skills are part of intellectual development; language is an essential part of the learning process.
2. Language has a vital role in understanding concepts.
3. The main foundations of language are constructed between the ages of 18 months and 4½ years, during which time the majority of children have fully integrated language as part of the thinking and learning process. It is easier to assist with language development and communication skills during this critical 3-year period than to sort out problems once children have reached school age.
4. Effective communication skills are essential for positive social interactions and emotional well-being. Communication difficulties can lead to isolation and frustration. Children who cannot communicate effectively may display emotional outbursts and/or aggressive, unwanted behaviour that can affect their development and learning in other areas.

(Kamen, 2000)

Identifying any areas where practitioners are concerned that a child may have a developmental delay, special educational need, or disability

All children have *individual* development and learning needs, but some may have *additional* or special needs that affect their ability to participate effectively in learning activities. For example, some children may not develop their intellectual processes in line with the expected pattern of development for their age for a variety of reasons: autistic spectrum disorders; attention deficit disorders; emotional difficulties; cognitive and learning difficulties.

All children have *individual* personal, social and emotional needs, but some may have *additional* or special needs that affect their ability to interact appropriately with others and/or participate effectively during routines and activities. For example, some children may have behavioural, social and/or emotional difficulties that hinder their ability to: follow specific routines or instructions for activities; interact positively with other children or adults; participate in play opportunities; express their feelings appropriately.

All children have *individual* communication and language needs, but some may have *additional* or special needs that affect their ability to communicate and interact effectively with others. For example: autistic spectrum disorders; behavioural and/or emotional difficulties; cognitive difficulties affecting the ability to process language; hearing impairment; physical disabilities affecting articulation of sounds. Depending on their individual language experiences, some children may not have reached the same level of language development as their peers or they may lack effective communication skills.

Some children may require additional support due to sensory and/or physical needs such as hearing, visual and/or physical impairment. As children with sensory or physical impairments may be dependent on others for some of their needs, it is essential to provide opportunities for them to be as independent as possible. Give them every chance to join in, to express opinions and to interact with their peer group.

Remember

Focus on each child as a unique person with individual strengths rather than focusing on the child's particular special needs or disabilities, i.e. focus what they can do rather than what they cannot.

There may be problems in interpreting needs, e.g. differences in the rate of development of children with similar background, disabilities, etc. Remember all children are unique individuals and develop at their own rate. Some children may be 'behind' in some areas of development but may 'catch up' with support from their parents/carers and the usual early years experiences (e.g. parent and toddler group, playgroup, nursery class) without the need for intervention.

However, some very young children may continue to experience difficulties even with input from skilled early years practitioners; these children and their parents may require additional or specialist support to maximise their development. It is important if early years practitioners are concerned about a child's behaviour, learning or development to contact the relevant support service. Such action may be part of Early Years Action Plus or statutory assessment (DfES, 2001).

Key guidelines

- In order to prepare for discussion with parents, it is important that practitioners review and reflect upon each child's development.
- If there are any concerns about a child's development then practitioners and parents should consider all contextual information about a child before taking any further steps. For example, has the arrival of a new sibling in the family caused a child to regress to younger patterns of behaviour? Are there signs that the child is about to make a developmental leap in this area?
- If any concerns are raised, this should be done on the basis of ongoing assessment observations of the child in a range of contexts in the setting and preferably also by the parents observing the child at home.
- Individual practitioners should not attempt to identify a special educational need (SEN) solely on the basis of their observations of the child within the setting. Identification must only be made by professionals or practitioners with specialist training.
- The progress check can be a useful part of the early identification process. Any concerns about a child's development should be discussed with the setting leader or manager and/or the setting's SENCO. Childminders should contact their childminding network or local authority officer for support.
- If there are concerns about a child's development in any particular area then a practitioner and the child's parents (in discussion with the setting leader, manager, childminding officer and/or the SENCO) may agree to draw up a plan to meet the child's needs within the setting and at home, then carry out a further review at an agreed date. This may include the need to work with other agencies.

(NCB, 2012, p.18)

You need to know and understand the details about particular disabilities or SEN as they affect the children in your setting and your ability to provide a high quality service. Children with special needs in your setting may include children with physical disabilities, behavioural difficulties, emotional difficulties, hearing impairment, visual impairment, communication difficulties and learning difficulties.

Families with children with disabilities who are referred for specialist support or seek help will have differing levels of need, ranging from advice, practical support and short-term intervention to detailed assessment and long-term intervention (DoH *et al.*, 2000). Examples of early interventions include: cognitive behaviour therapy; counselling; crisis intervention; family therapy; Home-Start; Portage; National Autistic Society Early Bird Programme; the Nippers Project (Nursery Intervention for Parents and Education Related Services); special nursery provision; Sure Start.

 Activity

- Investigate the types of special educational needs that may affect children. A useful starting point is ATL's *Achievement for All: Working with Children with Special Educational Needs in Mainstream Schools and Colleges* (2010). PDF available free from: **http://www.atl.org.uk/ Images/Achievment%20for%20all%20(2010).pdf**
- Find out about the early interventions available in your local area, e.g. counselling services, special nursery provision, Portage, Home-Start, and Sure Start.

Activities and strategies the practitioner intends to adopt to address any issues or concerns

As a practitioner you should help children with SEN or disabilities to participate in the full range of activities and experiences by: identifying and taking steps to overcome barriers to communication as well as identifying and taking steps to overcome barriers to participation in the full range of activities and experiences.

Ten ways to help young children with special needs to participate in activities

You can help young children with SEN or disabilities to participate in the full range of activities and experiences by:

1. Providing a stimulating, language-rich learning environment that is visually attractive, tactile and interactive.
2. Adapting the environment (e.g. the layout of furniture) and maximising the use of space in the setting to allow freedom of movement for *all* children (including those with physical disabilities or visual impairment).
3. Ensuring accessibility of materials and equipment.
4. Providing opportunities for all children to explore different materials and activities as well as offering alternative activities if appropriate.
5. Encouraging children to use the senses they have to their fullest extent.
6. Providing sufficient time for children to explore their environment and materials; some children may need extra time to complete tasks.
7. Implementing adaptations that can be made without the use of special aids and equipment and/or identifying and deploying specialist aids and equipment as necessary.
8. Encouraging independence, e.g. use of computers, word processing, tape recorders.
9. Praising *all* children's *efforts* as well as achievements.
10. Ensuring adults involved are knowledgeable about children's disabilities and special educational needs and are confident in their roles and responsibilities.

Figure 7.6 Practitioner supporting a young child with special needs

 **Activity**

Describe how you have supported young children with special educational needs.

Helping parents to support learning at home

Positive working relationships with parents are essential to provide continuity of care for very young children. Partnership between parents and childcarers depends on regular and open communication where contributions from both parties are acknowledged and valued. Friendly communication on a regular basis ensures continuity and consistency in providing shared routines and timing any necessary changes. Parents and practitioners can keep up to date with what a very young child has learned or is nearly ready to do through regular conversation, when they can exchange information and share delight about the child's discoveries and interests (Lindon, 2002).

As a practitioner you should support families in responding to their children's needs by working in partnership with parents. Establishing partnerships with parents is very important as parents are the child's primary carers and may have detailed specialist knowledge about their child. Parental involvement is crucial for both parents and practitioners as it:

- Increases parents' understanding of the learning process.
- Enables parents to reinforce tasks being undertaken by their child in the setting by engaging in similar activities with their child at home.

- Allows two-way communication between practitioners and parents.
- Enables shared knowledge about the individual child.
- Enhances the overall understanding of the child's needs in the setting and at home.

(Gatiss, 1991)

Most parents are keen to be actively involved in their children's learning. You should inform parents about the activities their child is involved in within the setting and suggest ways in which the parents can complement the work of the setting, such as:

- Encouraging family members to participate in observing and identifying the needs of children.
- Working through an agreed programme with an understanding of its steps towards progress, e.g. Portage schemes.
- Helping with individual and group activities in the setting, both indoors and outdoors.
- Supporting other professionals working with their child either in the setting or at home, e.g. physiotherapist, speech and language therapist.
- Assisting with activities outside the setting, e.g. outings to the local library, park, playground or swimming.

 Activity

Suggest practical ways to help parents support their children's learning at home. You could start by looking at useful materials to share with parents to support their understanding of the EYFS and how children learn through purposeful activity and play across all areas of development, which are available at **http://www.foundationyears.org.uk/**

Discussing with parents how the summary of development can be used to support learning at home

Practitioners must discuss with parents and/or carers how the summary of development can be used to support learning at home. Practitioners should encourage parents and/or carers to share information from the progress check with other relevant professionals, including their health visitor and/or a teacher (if a child moves to school-based provision at age 3). Practitioners must agree with parents and/or carers when will be the most useful point to provide a summary. It should be provided in time to inform the Healthy Child Programme health and development review at age 2 whenever possible (when health visitors gather information on a child's health and development, allowing them to identify any developmental delay and any particular support from which they think the child/family might benefit). Taking account of information from the progress check (which reflects ongoing, regular observation of children's development) should help ensure that health visitors can identify children's needs accurately and fully at the health review. Providers must have the consent of parents and/or carers to share information directly with other relevant professionals, if they consider this would be helpful (DfE, 2012, p.11).

Helping parents to understand the value of young children's play, and explaining to them what they are learning while they play, is a very important role for the early years practitioner. It helps parents to value their children's play at home and in the early years setting and will provide a good starting point for building up an effective partnership with parents (Thornton & Brunton, 2010a).

Parents and practitioners use this shared knowledge and understanding in order to plan together and think through ideas of how to move the child forward. Learning opportunities and next steps can be planned for the setting and the home. This process builds on what parents know and do already with their child, and supports their confidence and knowledge in how to extend and strengthen the early home learning environment (NCB, 2012, p.9).

As babies and young children explore the world they inhabit, they are naturally drawn to learning through playing and being playful. For young children, play is their work. Play engages children's bodies, minds and emotions, building up knowledge, skills and attitudes that will remain with them for the rest of their lives. In their play, children take control of their own learning by making choices, following preoccupations and interests, asking questions and practising their skills. They interact with others, learn how to manage their feelings and become confident about themselves and their abilities (Thornton & Brunton, 2010a).

 Activity

Take a look at the Thornton and Brunton article, 'The value of play in early years' (see Further reading), which includes useful ideas on play and learning at home to share with parents.

Encouraging parents to share the summary of progress with other relevant professionals

As a practitioner you should encourage parents to share the summary of progress with other relevant professionals – including their health visitor and/or a teacher (if a child moves to school-based provision at age 3). Practitioners must agree with parents and/or carers when will be the most useful point to provide a summary. It should be provided in time to inform the Healthy Child Programme health and development review at age 2 whenever possible (DfE, 2012, p.11).

Children with SEN may often have support from other professionals from external agencies. To provide the most effective care and support for children with SEN, it is essential that the working relationships between the setting staff and other professionals run smoothly and that there are no contradictions or missed opportunities due to lack of communication. Liaising with other professionals will enable you to involve colleagues with the work of the specialists in a number of ways, for example: planning appropriate support for the child within the setting; assisting children to perform tasks set by a specialist; reporting the child's progress on such tasks, e.g. to the child's parents.

Any interactions with other professionals should be conducted in such a way as to promote trust and confidence in your working relationships. Your contributions towards the planning and implementation of joint actions must be consistent with your role and responsibilities in your setting. You should supply other professionals with the relevant information, advice and support as appropriate to your own role and expertise. If requested, you should be willing to share information, knowledge or skills with other professionals. You should use any opportunities to contact or observe the practice of other professionals from external agencies to increase your knowledge and understanding of their skills/expertise in order to improve your own work (and that of your colleagues) in planning and supporting children's learning and development.

 Activity

1. Find out which external agencies and other professionals are connected with the care and support of young children with SEN at your setting.
2. Compile an information booklet that includes the following:
   - Links with other professionals from external agencies established by your setting.
   - A diagram that illustrates how you and your colleagues work with other professionals to provide effective support for children with SEN in your setting.
   - Your role and responsibilities in liaising with other professionals to support children with SEN and their parents.
   - Where to obtain information about the roles of other professionals in the local area.

Sharing information directly with health visitors with parental consent

As a practitioner you will need parental consent to share information directly with health visitors, which will help strengthen partnership working between services in order to support families.

Taking account of information from the progress check (which reflects ongoing, regular observation of children's development) should help ensure that health visitors can identify children's needs accurately and fully at the health review (when health visitors gather information on a child's health and development, allowing them to identify any developmental delay and any particular support from which they think the child/family might benefit). Providers must have the consent of parents and/or carers to share information directly with other relevant professionals, if they consider this would be helpful (DfE, 2012, p.11).

The progress check is a statutory requirement of the EYFS. Providers should seek the consent of parents to share information from the check directly with relevant professionals. Providers must have written policies and procedures in place to safeguard children, in line with the guidance and requirements of the relevant Local Safeguarding Children Board (LSCB) (NCB, 2012, p.15).

 Activity

Outline the procedures you use to help identify families in need of early intervention and support. Include information on how you:
- Communicate with children and their parents.
- Encourage families to discuss any concerns and to share information.
- Use different sources of information to identify concerns.
- Record information using agreed formats and confidentiality procedures.
- Refer concerns about children and families to the relevant agencies.

CHAPTER 8

The Early Years Foundation Stage Profile

This chapter provides you with useful information about the Early Years Foundation Stage Profile, including:

* The purpose of the Early Years Foundation Stage Profile
* The Early Learning Goals
* The key characteristics of effective learning.

Introduction

The Early Years Foundation Stage Profile is a statutory assessment for young children at the end of the Early Years Foundation Stage (EYFS) and is a way of summing up each child's development and learning at the end of the Reception year.

The purpose of the Early Years Foundation Stage Profile

The main purpose of the EYFS Profile is to provide a reliable, valid and accurate assessment of individual young children at the end of the EYFS. The Profile describes each child's attainment against the 17 Early Learning Goals (see below) together with a short written account about their learning characteristics (see section below, 'The key characteristics of effective learning').

The new EYFS Profile is intended to be used as a summative assessment completed at the end of the Reception year. Schools will need to consider their approaches to day-to-day assessment and materials to support this, referring to the Development Matters in the Early Years Foundation Stage bands for guidance (see Further reading). The revised EYFS Profile came into effect in September 2012.

The Profile report must reflect ongoing observation

The Profile report must reflect ongoing observation and take account of all relevant records held by the setting including discussions with parents and other relevant adults. In the final term of the year in which the child reaches age 5, and no later than 30 June in that term, the EYFS Profile must be completed for each child. The Profile provides parents and carers, practitioners and teachers with a well-rounded picture of a child's knowledge, understanding and abilities, their progress against expected levels, and their readiness for Year 1. The Profile must reflect: ongoing observation; all relevant records held by the setting; discussions with parents and carers, and any other adults whom the teacher, parent or carer judges can offer a useful contribution (DfE, 2012, p.11).

The Government does not prescribe how ongoing assessment should be undertaken. In addition to the statutory framework, an updated version of the non-statutory guidance, Development Matters in the Early Years Foundation Stage, was published alongside the EYFS in March 2012. Early years providers may find this useful in making any assessment judgements about children, before undertaking the EYFS Profile.

Activity

- Find out about your setting's policy and procedures relating to observation and assessment at the end of the EYFS.
- Find out about the sequences of development for children in the last year of the EYFS.

Providing parents, practitioners and teachers with a well-rounded picture of the child

Young children require holistic opportunities to develop a wide range of skills covering all aspects of their development, e.g. social, physical, intellectual, communication and emotional. These opportunities should be provided throughout the early years and continue in the school years and into adult life. Such opportunities should be presented in a play-based, hands-on framework for learning, where young children can explore and experiment. Every child should be treated as a unique individual and provided with age- and development-appropriate learning opportunities to suit their specific needs, through a mix of child-initiated and adult-led activities. (See 'Child-initiated activity and adult-led activity' in Chapter 5.)

The EYFS Profile should provide parents, practitioners and teachers with a well-rounded picture of each child's knowledge, understanding and abilities, including their progress against expected levels (the Early Learning Goals) and their readiness for school. The EYFS promotes teaching and learning to ensure children's 'school readiness' and gives children the broad range of knowledge and skills that provide the right foundation for good future progress through school and life (DfE, 2012, p.2).

Schools (or other relevant providers) must share the results of the EYFS Profile with parents and/ or carers, and explain to them when and how they can discuss the Profile with the teacher (or other practitioner) who completed it. For children attending more than one setting, the Profile must be completed by the school where the child spends the most time. If a child moves to a new school during the academic year, the original school must send their assessment of the child's level of development against the Early Learning Goals to the new school within 15 days of receiving a request. If a child moves during the summer term, relevant providers must agree which of them will complete the Profile (DfE, 2012, pp.11–12).

The EYFS Profile must be completed for all children, including those with special educational needs or disabilities. Reasonable adjustments to the assessment process for children with special educational needs and disabilities must be made as appropriate. Providers should consider whether they may need to seek specialist assistance to help them with this. Children will have differing levels of skills and abilities across the Profile and it is important that there is a full assessment of all areas of their development, to inform plans for future activities and to identify any additional support needs (DfE, 2012, p.12).

Helping teachers to plan activities for children starting Key Stage 1

Year 1 teachers must be given a copy of the Profile report together with a short commentary on each child's skills and abilities in relation to the three key characteristics of effective learning (see below). These should inform a dialogue between Reception and Year 1 teachers about each child's stage of development and learning needs and assist with the planning of activities in Year 1 (DfE, 2012, p.11).

The continuity in learning for children as they progress from home and pre-school through Reception into Years 1 and 2 is an unusually difficult transition for children in England – in particular, the change from learning through play to formal classroom teaching comes earlier, and more abruptly, in England than in most other countries. Many practitioners believe that Key Stage 1 needs to be adapted to the EYFS rather than the other way round. It is vital for Key Stage 1 to demonstrate continuity with the EYFS because this would allow for the development of skills through play-based learning rather than an emphasis on knowledge; this approach would enable teachers to introduce and practise literacy, numeracy and scientific skills in a context that would interest and stimulate children.

The EYFS places the emphasis on personal development through three prime areas of learning (personal, social and emotional development; communication and language; physical development) that provide the foundations for young children's ability to learn and develop healthily. The basic skills acquired in these areas are applied in four specific areas of learning that prepare the way for literacy, mathematics, expressive arts and design, and understanding the world. Key Stage 1 should continue the theme of personal development, extend and deepen it, and create a bridge towards the subject knowledge-based curriculum that is the main focus of secondary education.

The Early Learning Goals

The new Early Years Foundation Stage Profile is used to assess development at the end of the Reception year using significantly fewer Early Learning Goals – a reduction from 69 to 17. Each child's level of development must be assessed against the Early Learning Goals (DfE, 2012, p.11).

Achieving the Early Learning Goals

Practitioners must indicate whether children are meeting expected levels of development (i.e. achieved the Early Learning Goals), or if they are exceeding expected levels, or not yet reaching expected levels.

Early Learning Goals

Personal, social and emotional development	Emerging	Expected	Exceeding
Self-confidence and self-awareness	Children join in a range of activities that interest them. They are confident to talk to other children when playing together. They can talk about what they need and what they enjoy doing, and make choices about the activities they prefer. They select and use resources with support.	Children are confident to try new activities, and say why they like some activities more than others. They are confident to speak in a familiar group, will talk about their ideas, and will choose the resources they need for their chosen activities. They say when they do or don't need help.	Children are confident to speak to a class group. They can talk about the things they enjoy and are good at, and about the things they don't find easy. They are resourceful in finding support when they need help or information. They can talk about the plans they have made to carry out activities and what they might change if they were to repeat them.
Managing feelings and behaviour	Children are aware of their own feelings and know that some actions and words can hurt the feelings of others. They can take turns and share, sometimes with support from others. They can usually adapt their behaviour to different events, social situations and changes in routines.	Children talk about how they and others show feelings, talk about their own and others' behaviour and its consequences, and know that some behaviour is unacceptable. They work as part of a group or class, and understand and follow the rules. They adjust their behaviour to different situations, and take changes of routine in their stride.	Children know some ways to manage their feelings and are beginning to use these to maintain control. They can listen to each other's suggestions and plan how to achieve an outcome without adult help. They know when and how to stand up for themselves appropriately. They can stop and think before acting and they can wait for things they want.

(Continued)

Early Learning Goals

	Emerging	Expected	Exceeding
Making relationships	Children play as part of a group and know how to make friends with others. They show some awareness of other children's needs.	Children play co-operatively, taking turns with others. They take account of one another's ideas about how to organise their activity. They show sensitivity to others' needs and feelings, and form positive relationships with adults and other children.	Children play group games with rules. They understand someone else's point of view can be different from theirs. They resolve minor disagreements through listening to each other to come up with a fair solution. They understand what bullying is and that this is unacceptable behaviour.
Physical development			
Moving and handling	Children can maintain balance when they concentrate. They run skilfully and negotiate space successfully, adjusting speed or direction to avoid obstacles. They are beginning to hold a pencil or crayon with thumb and two fingers.	Children show good control and co-ordination in large and small movements. They move confidently in a range of ways, safely negotiating space. They handle equipment and tools effectively, including pencils for writing.	Children can hop confidently and skip in time to music. They hold paper in position and use their preferred hand for writing, using correct pencil grip. They are beginning to be able to write on lines and control letter size.
Health and self-care	Children can tell adults when they are hungry or tired or when they want to rest or play. They can dress with some assistance and can usually manage personal needs such as washing their hands and toileting.	Children know the importance for good health of physical exercise and a healthy diet, and talk about ways to keep healthy and safe. They manage their own basic hygiene and personal needs successfully, including dressing and going to the toilet independently.	Children know about and can make healthy choices in relation to eating and exercise. They can dress and undress independently, successfully managing fastening buttons or laces.

Communication and language	Emerging	Expected	Exceeding
Listening and attention	Children listen to others one-to-one or in small groups when the conversation interests them. When listening to familiar stories and rhymes children can join in at relevant points with repeated refrains and phrases and can anticipate key events. They can focus their attention by shifting between an activity and listening.	Children listen attentively in a range of situations. They listen to stories, accurately anticipating key events and respond to what they hear with relevant comments, questions or actions. They give their attention to what others say and respond appropriately, while engaged in another activity.	Children listen to instructions and follow them accurately, asking for clarification if necessary. They listen attentively with sustained concentration to follow a story without pictures or props and can listen in a larger group, for example at assembly.
Understanding	Children respond to instructions when, for example, they are asked to get or put away an item, and understand the meaning of words such as 'on' and 'under'. They can identify familiar objects by the way in which they are used.	Children follow instructions involving several ideas or actions. They answer 'how' and 'why' questions about their experiences and in response to stories or events.	After listening to stories children can express views about the events or characters in the story and answer questions about why things happened. They can carry out instructions that contain several parts in a sequence.
Speaking	Children can connect ideas using talk, actions or objects and can retell a simple past event in the correct order. They question why things happen and give simple explanations.	Children express themselves effectively, showing awareness of listeners' needs. They use past, present and future forms accurately when talking about events that have happened or are going to happen in the future. They develop their own narratives and explanations by connecting ideas or events.	Children show some awareness of the listener by making changes to language and non-verbal features. They recount experiences and imagine possibilities, often connecting ideas. They use a range of vocabulary in imaginative ways to add information, express ideas or to explain or justify actions or events.

(Continued)

Early Learning Goals

Literacy	Emerging	Expected	Exceeding
Reading	Children know that print carries meaning. They show an interest in books and can suggest how a story might end. They can segment the sounds in simple words and blend them together, and join in with rhyming and rhythmic activities.	Children read and understand simple sentences. They use phonic knowledge to decode regular words and read them aloud accurately. They also read some common irregular words. They demonstrate understanding when talking with others about what they have read.	Children can read phonically regular words of more than one syllable as well as many irregular but high frequency words. They use phonic, semantic and syntactic knowledge to understand unfamiliar vocabulary. They can describe the main events in the simple stories they have read.
Writing	Children give meaning to marks they make as they paint, draw and write. They can segment words orally, and use some clearly identifiable letters to communicate meaning, representing some sounds correctly and in sequence.	Children use their phonic knowledge to write words in ways that match their spoken sounds. They also write some irregular common words. They write simple sentences that can be read by themselves and others. Some words are spelt correctly and others are phonetically plausible.	Children can spell phonically regular words of more than one syllable as well as many irregular but high frequency words. They use key features of narrative in their own writing.
Numbers	Children match and compare the numbers of objects in two groups of up to five objects, recognising when the sets contain the same number of objects. They show curiosity about numbers by offering comments or asking questions. They find one more or less from a group of up to five objects.	Children count reliably with numbers from one to 20, place them in order and say which number is one more or one less than a given number. Using quantities and objects, they add and subtract two single-digit numbers and count on or back to find the answer. They solve problems, including doubling, halving and sharing.	Children estimate a number of objects and check quantities by counting up to 10. They solve practical problems that involve combining groups of two, five or ten, or sharing into equal groups.

Shape, space and measures	Children identify and describe shapes in simple models, pictures and patterns. They can compare properties of objects that are 'big' or 'small', or their position in relation to one another, such as whether one is 'behind' or 'next to' another.	Children use everyday language to talk about size, weight, capacity, position, distance, time and money to compare quantities and objects and to solve problems. They recognise, create and describe patterns. They explore characteristics of everyday objects and shapes and use mathematical language to describe them.	Children estimate, measure, weigh and compare and order objects and talk about properties, position and time.
Understanding the world	Emerging	Expected	Exceeding
People and communities	Children can recognise some special times or events in their lives and the lives of others. They know some of the things that make them unique, and can talk about some of the ways they are similar to, or different from, their friends or family.	Children talk about past and present events in their own lives and in the lives of family members. They know that other children don't always enjoy the same things, and are sensitive to this. They know about similarities and differences between themselves and others, and between families, communities and traditions.	Children know the difference between past and present events in their own lives and some reasons why people's lives were different in the past. They know that other children have different likes and dislikes and that they may be good at different things. They understand that different people have different beliefs, attitudes, customs and traditions and why it is important to treat them with respect.

(Continued)

Early Learning Goals

The world	Children show an interest in aspects of their familiar world such as the place where they live or the environment. They are curious about and interested in why things happen and how things work. They can talk about some of the things they have observed such as plants, animals, natural and found objects.	Children know about similarities and differences in relation to places, objects, materials and living things. They talk about the features of their own immediate environment and how environments might vary from one another. They make observations of animals and plants and explain why some things occur, and talk about changes.	Children know that the environment and living things are influenced by human activity. They can describe some actions that people in their own community do to help maintain the area they live in. They know the properties of some materials and can suggest some of the purposes for which they are used. They are familiar with basic scientific concepts, such as floating, sinking, experimentation.
Technology	Children show an interest in technological toys with knobs or pulleys, or real objects such as cameras and mobile phones. They show skill in making toys work by pressing parts or lifting flaps to achieve effects such as sound, movement or new images.	Children recognise that a range of technology is used in places such as homes and schools. They select and use technology for particular purposes.	Children use a range of everyday technology. They select appropriate applications that support an identified need – for example deciding how best to make a record of a special event in their lives, such as a journey on a steam train.

Expressive arts and design	Emerging	Expected	Exceeding
Explore and use media and materials	Children imitate and create movement in response to music, join in dancing games and sing a few familiar songs. They explore and differentiate between colours, begin to describe the texture of things, and create 3D structures.	Children sing songs, make music and dance, and experiment with ways of changing them; safely use and explore a variety of materials, tools and techniques, experimenting with colour, design, texture, form and function.	Children develop their own ideas through selecting and using materials and working on processes that interest them. Through their explorations they find out and make decisions about how media and materials can be combined and changed.
Be imaginative	Children create simple representations of events, people and objects. They sing to themselves, explore sounds, and tap out simple repeated rhythms. They engage in imaginative play and role play based on their experiences.	Children use what they have learnt about media and materials in original ways, thinking about uses and purposes; they represent their own ideas, thoughts and feelings through design and technology, art, music, dance, role play and stories.	Children talk about the ideas and processes that have led them to make music, designs, images or products. They can talk about features of their own and other's work, recognising the differences between them and the strengths of each.

Table 8.1 EYFS Profile: Early Learning Goals (Bertram & Pascal, 2012)

 **Activity**

Observe a group of children aged 4 to 5 years during a play activity or playing a game. Focus on one child's personal, social and emotional development. In your assessment comment on:

- The child's self-confidence and self-awareness.
- The child's ability to make relationships.
- The child's ability to manage their feelings and behaviour.
- The role of the adult in promoting the child's personal, social and emotional development.
- Suggestions for further activities to encourage or extend the child's personal, social and emotional development, including appropriate resources.

Figure 8.1 The Early Learning Goals in physical development

 **Activity**

Observe a group of children aged 4 to 5 years during an indoor movement session or outdoor play. Focus on one child's physical development. In your assessment comment on:

- The child's movements and ability to handle equipment.
- The child's understanding of healthy diet and exercise.
- The child's ability to manage their own self-care.
- The role of the adult in promoting the child's physical development.
- Suggestions for further activities to encourage or extend the child's physical development, including appropriate resources.

 **Activity**

Observe a group of children aged 4 to 5 years involved in a discussion or circle time. Focus on one child's communication skills and language development. In your assessment comment on:

- The child's ability to listen and pay attention.
- The child's ability to understand instructions and answer questions.
- The child's ability to express themselves.
- The role of the adult in promoting the child's communication skills and language development.
- Suggestions for further activities to encourage or extend the child's communication skills and language development, including appropriate resources.

Figure 8.2 The Early Learning Goals in communication and language

Figure 8.3 The Early Learning Goals in literacy

 Activity

Observe a group of children aged 4 to 5 years involved in a literacy activity. Focus on one child's literacy development. In your assessment comment on:

- The child's reading skills.
- The child's writing skills.
- The role of the adult in promoting the child's literacy development.
- Suggestions for further activities to encourage or extend the child's literacy development, including appropriate resources.

 Activity

Observe a group of children aged 4 to 5 years involved in a mathematics activity. Focus on one child's mathematics development. In your assessment comment on:

- The child's understanding of numbers.
- The child's understanding of shape, space and measures.
- The role of the adult in promoting the child's mathematics development.
- Suggestions for further activities to encourage or extend the child's mathematics development, including appropriate resources.

Figure 8.4 The Early Learning Goals in mathematics

 Activity

Observe a group of children aged 4 to 5 years involved in a science activity. Focus on one child's development in understanding the world. In your assessment comment on:

- The child's understanding of people and communities.
- The child's understanding of the world.
- The child's understanding of technology.
- The role of the adult in promoting the child's development in understanding the world.
- Suggestions for further activities to encourage or extend the child's development in understanding the world, including appropriate resources.

Figure 8.5 The Early Learning Goals in understanding the world: communities

Figure 8.6 The Early Learning Goals in expressive arts and design

 **Activity**

Observe a group of children aged 4 to 5 years involved in an art, drama or music activity. Focus on one child's development in the expressive arts and design. In your assessment comment on:

● The child's ability to explore and use media and materials.
● The child's ability to be imaginative.
● The child's understanding of technology.
● The role of the adult in promoting the child's development in the expressive arts and design.
● Suggestions for further activities to encourage or extend the child's development in the expressive arts and design, including appropriate resources.

 Activity

● Look back at your observations and assessments of a child's development in this chapter.
● For each aspect of development, identify whether the child has achieved the 'expected' development (e.g. Early Learning Goal) or if their development is 'emerging' or 'exceeding' the expected development.

The key characteristics of effective learning

In planning and guiding children's activities, practitioners must reflect on the different ways that children learn and reflect these in practice. Three characteristics of effective teaching and learning are:

● **Playing and exploring** – children investigate and experience things, and 'have a go'.
● **Active learning** – children concentrate and keep on trying if they encounter difficulties, and enjoy achievements.
● **Creating and thinking critically** – children have and develop their own ideas, make links between ideas, and develop strategies for doing things.

(DfE, 2012, pp.6–7)

Intellectual stimulation through play and other learning opportunities allows children to develop their cognitive abilities and fulfil their potential as individuals.

Child's name:_____ Age in months:_____

Area of learning	Aspect	Emerging	Expected	Exceeding
Personal, Social and Emotional Development	Self-confidence and self-awareness			
	Managing feelings and behaviour			
	Making relationships			
Physical Development	Moving and handling			
	Health and self-care			
Communication and Language	Listening and attention			
	Understanding			
	Speaking			
Literacy	Reading			
	Writing			
Mathematics	Numbers			
	Shape, space and measures			
Understanding the World	People and communities			
	The world			
	Technology			
Expressive Arts and Design	Exploring and using media and materials			
	Being imaginative			

Figure 8.7 Example of EYFS Profile

The children you work with will be constantly thinking and learning, e.g. gathering new information and formulating new ideas about themselves, other people and the world around them.

When planning and guiding children's activities, you should provide children with opportunities to:

- Explore their environment and/or investigate new information/ideas.
- Discover things for themselves through a wide variety of experiences.
- Feel free to make mistakes in a safe and secure environment using 'trial and error'.
- Develop autonomy through increased responsibility and working independently.
- Encourage and extend their knowledge and skills with appropriate support from adults (and other children).
- Learn to make sense of new information within an appropriate curriculum framework.

The ways in which young children engage with other people and their environment – playing and exploring, active learning, and creating and thinking critically – underpin learning and development across all areas and support the children to remain effective and motivated learners. Children develop in the context of relationships and the environment around them. This context is unique to each family, and reflects individual communities and cultures (Early Education, 2012, p.4).

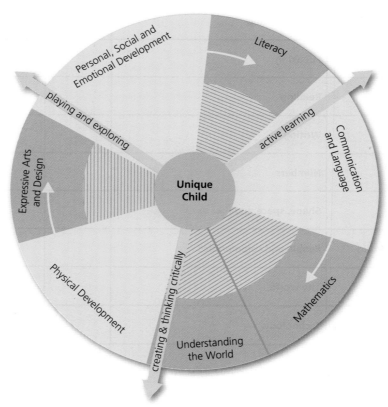

Figure 8.8 The unique child reaches out to relate to people and things through the characteristics of effective learning, which move through all areas of learning (Early Education, 2012, *Development Matters in the Early Years Foundation Stage (EYFS)*, p.4)

Characteristics of effective learning

Playing and exploring – engagement

Finding out and exploring

- Showing curiosity about objects, events and people
- Using senses to explore the world around them
- Engaging in open-ended activity
- Showing particular interests.

Playing with what they know

- Pretending objects are things from their experience
- Representing their experiences in play
- Taking on a role in their play
- Acting out experiences with other people.

Being willing to 'have a go'

- Initiating activities
- Seeking challenge
- Showing a 'can do' attitude
- Taking a risk, engaging in new experiences, and learning by trial and error.

Active learning – motivation

Being involved and concentrating

- Maintaining focus on their activity for a period of time
- Showing high levels of energy, fascination
- Not easily distracted
- Paying attention to details.

Keeping trying

- Persisting with activity when challenges occur
- Showing a belief that more effort or a different approach will pay off
- Bouncing back after difficulties.

Enjoying achieving what they set out to do

- Showing satisfaction in meeting their own goals
- Being proud of how they accomplished something – not just the end result
- Enjoying meeting challenges for their own sake rather than external rewards or praise.

Creating and thinking critically – thinking

Having their own ideas

- Thinking of ideas
- Finding ways to solve problems
- Finding new ways to do things.

(Continued)

Characteristics of effective learning
Making links
• Making links and noticing patterns in their experience • Making predictions • Testing their ideas • Developing ideas of grouping, sequence, cause and effect.
Choosing ways to do things
• Planning, making decisions about how to approach a task, solve a problem and reach a goal • Checking how well their activities are going • Changing strategy as needed • Reviewing how well the approach worked.

Table 8.2 Adapted from Stewart, N., *How Children Learn: The Characteristics of Effective Early Learning* (Early Education, 2011, p.107)

Playing and exploring

Babies and young children are powerful learners, reaching out into the world and making sense of their experiences with other people, objects and events. As they explore and learn, children are naturally drawn to play. Play and exploration have a central role within close, respectful relationships to support early development. Practitioners with children of nursery and Reception age sometimes feel uncertain about providing an appropriate combination of child-initiated and adult-led activities, and balancing open-ended play and exploration and direct teaching in adult-led activities. The EYFS and the Early Learning Goals (ELGs), however, provide sufficient flexibility for practitioners to follow children's interests, respond to their ideas for developing play activities, and provide structured activities (which can also be playful) to teach specific knowledge and skills (DCSF/QCDA, 2009, pp.3–4).

The best outcomes for children's learning occur where most of the activity within a child's day is a mixture of child-initiated play that is actively supported by adults, and focused learning, with adults guiding the learning through playful, rich experiential activities. As part of this general emphasis on combining child-initiated play and playful adult-led opportunities, confident and reflective practitioners will select the approach that is best for the developmental stage of the children, and for individuals and groups. For example, within a whole day it may be that a period of free play without adult involvement meets a child's need for space, independence and relaxation. This may apply particularly in an out-of-school club, for example, or for children attending settings for full days. On the other hand, short sessions of carefully planned, structured activity can be useful in teaching specific skills, for example benefiting children with identified special educational needs, building vocabulary for children learning English as an additional language or demonstrating how to use tools or equipment (DCSF/QCDA, 2009, p.5). (There is more information about child-initiated and adult-led activities in Chapter 5.)

Active learning

An essential part of all learning experiences is active participation or active learning. Not just for children but for adults as well. For example, at college you may find that learning situations take the form of workshops, group activities and discussions rather than formal lectures. Children (and adults) learn by *doing*. Lectures would be a waste of time for children. Indeed, traditional lectures *are* a waste of time, even for adults! This is because the average attention-span of an adult is 20 minutes! (This is probably why commercials are shown about every 15 to 20 minutes on television.) The average attention span of a child is considerably less, more like 5 to 10 minutes or even as little as 2 to 3 minutes, especially for very young children, some children with cognitive difficulties or behavioural difficulties.

Key Term

Active learning: learning by doing; participation in activities in meaningful situations.

In all learning situations it is important to provide information in small portions with plenty of discussion and activity breaks to maintain interest and concentration. It is essential that children become *actively* involved in the learning process. Learning needs to be practical not theoretical. Children need *concrete* learning experiences, e.g. using real objects in a meaningful context. This is why providing appropriate play opportunities is so crucial to all children's learning and development. Active learning encourages children to be:

- **C**urious
- **H**andy at problem solving
- **I**maginative
- **C**reative.

Theories of learning and development agree with these perspectives from brain research. Learning is both individual and social. Young children are not passive learners – they enjoy participating in 'hands-on' and 'brains-on' activities. They actively drive their own learning and development, by the choices they make, the interests they develop, the questions they ask, the knowledge they seek, and their motivation to act more competently. Children's choices and interests are the driving force for building knowledge, skills and understanding: by working and playing with other people, they are constantly learning about themselves and their social and cultural worlds. Children build positive identities through collaborative, caring relationships with other people, by managing and taking risks, 'having a go', experiencing success, developing resilience, and developing 'mastery' and 'can-do' attitudes. High-quality provision helps children to develop positive dispositions that lay the foundations for becoming lifelong successful learners (DCSF/QCDA, 2009, p.6).

Creating and thinking critically

Creating and thinking critically involves: using intellectual processes to make personal judgements; making connections between existing information and new information; problem solving and the ability to think logically. People use their existing knowledge and past experiences to solve problems. Children (and adults) often supplement their lack of knowledge or experience by experimenting using a process of trial and error. Making mistakes is part of the learning process. By using logic, people can make reasonable assumptions or predictions about what might happen in a particular situation or to a particular object. Logical thinking and problem solving are essential to the ability to make mathematical calculations and to develop scientific skills. Children need lots of opportunities to develop these scientific skills: observation; investigation; prediction; hypothesising; recording data.

There should be a balance between encouraging younger children to develop their own problem solving skills through play with minimal adult intervention, and complying with the Early Learning Goals for mathematics and understanding the world.

Adults play a crucial role in providing opportunities and experiences that enable children to develop their thinking skills. Practitioners working with babies and young children need to teach, explain, demonstrate, model, scaffold and support. More importantly, they need to give children the time and space to experiment with the knowledge and skills they have experienced, in order to discover for themselves. Children need to feel secure enough to make mistakes in a culture where mistakes are seen as a means of discovery not failure (Clarke, 2008).

Thinking takes time, concentration and perseverance; therefore children need to be motivated, which is more likely in a play situation, as here they feel they have choice and control. Child-initiated learning creates the right motivation and opportunity for developing thinking skills as it incorporates the key elements of time, choice, value, and opportunities to think about 'what, how, when, why and next time', along with quality adult input and support. For the adults this is an ideal time to find out what the children know, how they use their knowledge and what might be needed to encourage more thinking (Clarke, 2008).

Imagination involves the individual's ability to invent ideas or to form images. Children express their imagination through imitative play to begin with and then gradually through imaginative play, e.g. pretend play or role play. As children explore their environment and find out what objects and materials can do, they use their imagination to increase their understanding of the world and their role within it. For example, through imaginative play children can become other people by dressing up and behaving like them. Imaginative play assists the development of children's imagination through activities such as dressing up, small-scale toys, doll play, shop play and hospital play.

 Key Term

Imagination: the individual's ability to invent ideas or to form images.

Creativity is the use of the imagination in a wide variety of activities, including play, art, design technology, music, dance, drama, stories and poetry. Children can express their creativity through creative activities, such as painting, drawing, collage, playdough, clay, cooking, design and model making. Creativity involves a process rather than an end product; it cannot be measured by the end result of an activity, but is based upon *how* the child worked and *why*. Creativity involves: exploring and experimenting with a wide range of materials; learning about the properties of materials, e.g. colour, shape, size and texture; developing fine motor skills to manipulate materials; developing problem solving techniques; developing an understanding of the world and our personal contribution to it.

Key Term

Creativity: the use of the imagination in a wide variety of activities, including play, art, design technology, music, dance, drama, stories and poetry.

Practitioners have a key role in building the right conditions for learning. Firstly and fundamentally, adults ensure that children feel known and valued as individuals, and feel safe and cared for. Their own rate of development is respected, so that children are not rushed but are supported in ways that are right for each child. Children's time must be managed so that they have the opportunity to become deeply involved in their activities and to follow their ideas through, including returning later to continue their explorations or creative expressions. Adults manage the pace of activities, planning varied and interesting new experiences to stimulate learning alongside opportunities for children to revisit, practise or enjoy a sense of mastery. With this groundwork in place, it is then the adult's skilled interactions that will move learning forward (DCSF/QCDA, 2009, p.6).

A short commentary on each child's skills and abilities in relation to the three key characteristics of effective learning

The commentary on each child's skills and abilities in relation to the three key characteristics of effective learning should include information gathered from your ongoing observations and assessments. For example, comment on the child's abilities in relation to:

Playing and exploring

- Play both indoors and out, alone and with others, quietly or boisterously.
- Find out about things, try out and practise ideas and skills, take risks, explore their feelings, learn from mistakes.
- Be in control and think imaginatively.

Active learning

- Learn and remember things by taking experiences in through the senses as they move.
- Use all their senses to explore in real hands-on activities.
- Put the information together in their own minds to form ideas and make sense of the world.

Creating and thinking critically

- Use out-loud thinking to clarify their thoughts, regulate their activities, take on imaginative roles and rehearse their skills.
- Work out what to do, try hard, persevere with problems.
- Find out and think for themselves to develop real understanding through challenges that may occur in play, in real life or planned activities.

Name Age Date	Key person's signature Moderated by	Parent's/carer's signature/comments

Your child's learning

Playing and exploring – *finding out and exploring; playing with what they know; being willing to 'have a go'.*
Active learning – *being involved and concentrating; keeping trying; enjoying achieving what they set out to do.*
Creating and thinking critically – *having their own ideas; making links; choosing ways to do things.*

Personal, Social and Emotional Development *Making relationships; self-confidence and self-awareness; managing feelings and behaviour*	**Communication and Language** *Listening and attention; understanding; speaking*	**Physical Development** *Moving and handling; health and self-care*
Making relationships	**Listening and attention**	**Moving and handling**
0–11 8–20 16–26 22–36 30–50 40–60+	0–11 8–20 16–26 22–36 30–50 40–60+	0–11 8–20 16–26 22–36 30–50 40–60+
Self-confidence and self-awareness	**Understanding**	**Health and self-care**
0–11 8–20 16–26 22–36 30–50 40–60+	0–11 8–20 16–26 22–36 30–50 40–60+	0–11 8–20 16–26 22–36 30–50 40–60+
Managing feelings and behaviour	**Speaking**	
0–11 8–20 16–26 22–36 30–50 40–60+	0–11 8–20 16–26 22–36 30–50 40–60+	

Literacy *Reading; writing*	**Mathematics** *Numbers; shape, space and measure*	**Understanding the World** *People and communities; the world; technology*	**Expressive Arts and Design** *Exploring and using media and materials; being imaginative*
Reading	**Numbers**	**People and communities**	**Exploring and using media and materials**
0–11 8–20 16–26 22–36 30–50 40–60+	0–11 8–20 16–26 22–36 30–50 40–60+	0–11 8–20 16–26 22–36 30–50 40–60+	0–11 8–20 16–26 22–36 30–50 40–60+
Writing	**Shape, space and measure**	**The world**	**Being imaginative**
0–11 8–20 16–26 22–36 30–50 40–60+	0–11 8–20 16–26 22–36 30–50 40–60+	0–11 8–20 16–26 22–36 30–50 40–60+	0–11 8–20 16–26 22–36 30–50 40–60+
		Technology	
		0–11 8–20 16–26 22–36 30–50 40–60+	

Figure 8.9 EYFS Transition Report (http://www.qed.uk.com/trackers.htm – see Further reading)

Activity

Look back at your observations and assessments of individual children's development in this chapter. Provide a short commentary on each child's skills and abilities in relation to the three key characteristics of effective learning:

● Playing and exploring – children investigate and experience things, and 'have a go'.
● Active learning – children concentrate and keep on trying if they encounter difficulties, and enjoy achievements.
● Creating and thinking critically – children have and develop their own ideas, make links between ideas, and develop strategies for doing things.

Glossary

Active learning: learning by doing; participation in activities in meaningful situations.

Auditory perception: the processing and interpretation of sound as meaningful information.

Behaviour: a person's actions, reactions and treatment of others.

Contexts: these are made up of people and provision. They create both the access to learning and the ethos in which the child learns.

Creativity: the *use* of the imagination in a wide variety of activities, including play, art, design technology, music, dance, drama, stories and poetry.

Cross-sectional observation: method of observation used to compare developmental levels at various ages or backgrounds.

Emotional outbursts: uncontrolled expressions of intense emotion, e.g. rage or frustration.

Ethos: the characteristic spirit of a group of people or community, e.g. a happy ethos and/or a caring ethos.

Event sample: an observer makes notes on a child's/children's actions and interactions. There is no fixed time at which these notes are made; the frequency of the event determines the amount of information gathered.

Evidence: anything that shows the child's progress, e.g. what the child said or did or made.

Field notes: (or anecdotal notes) notes containing text and pictures that deal with the daily activities of children and observations by practitioners in the setting. They can record specific milestones, skills attained and progression or digression of certain skills.

Holistic: looking at the 'whole' child or young person, i.e. *all* aspects of the child's or young person's development – social and emotional, physical, intellectual, communication and language.

Imagination: the individual's ability to invent ideas or to form images.

Information sharing protocol: a signed agreement between two or more organisations or bodies, in relation to specified information sharing activity and/or arrangements for the routine of bulk sharing of personal information.

Key person: the member of staff with whom a child has more contact than other adults within the setting; this adult demonstrates a special interest in the child (and their family) through close daily interaction.

Longitudinal study: carrying out regular observations over a long period of time, for example observing a child's development and progress over a few weeks, months or even years.

Mapping: also known as movement or tracking charts. A rapid method of noting a child's movements during a set period by adding arrows and times to a room layout sketch.

Milestones: significant skills that children develop in and around certain ages as part of the usual or expected pattern of development.

Norm: the usual pattern or expected level of development/behaviour.

Objective: only recording what we *actually* see and hear.

Observation schedule: an analytical form, or coding sheet, filled in by a practitioner that specifies categories of behaviours under scrutiny. Observations are coded and later aggregated into quantifiable data.

Participant observation: enabling researchers to learn about the activities of the children under study in the natural setting through observing and participating in those activities.

Profile: evidence gathered together to create a picture of each child's learning and development, including observations and assessments.

Regression: demonstrating behaviour characteristic of a previous level of development.

Running record: a written description of a child's behaviour – what the child says or does is in sequence.

Scaffolding: adult assistance given to support the child's thinking and learning, as the child develops competence the adult decreases support until the child works independently.

Schemas: term used mainly by Piaget and Froebel to describe internal thought processes.

Self-concept: how children feel about themselves.

Sequences: development following the same basic pattern but not necessarily at fixed ages.

Significant moment: a leap in a child's learning or development or progress.

Social context: any situation or environment where social interaction occurs, e.g. home, early years setting, local community.

Special educational needs: all children have *individual* needs, but some children may have *additional* needs due to physical disability, sensory impairment, communication or social interaction difficulties, learning difficulties or emotional/behavioural difficulties.

Stages: development that occurs at fixed ages.

Structured recording system: observing and recording for a specific reason (for example a child's ability to complete a specific task such as drawing a person) using pre-printed sheets.

Subjective: recording our *interpretation* of what we see and hear.

Target child observation: also known as coded observation, this focuses on one child by collecting data on a prepared record sheet using abbreviations or codes.

Time sample: an observer makes notes of a child's or group of children's actions and interactions at regular intervals over a set period of time.

Visual perception: the ability to process and interpret information using the eyes.

Zone of proximal development: Vygotsky's description for a child's next area of development where adult assistance is only required until the child has developed the skill and can do it independently.

Further reading
Websites

Birth to Five Development Timeline – this interactive guide is really helpful (especially if you are new to childcare) as it shows the milestones in a child's development from birth to 5 years old: http://www.nhs.uk/Tools/Pages/birthtofive.aspx?Tag=Interactive+timelines

Birth to Three Matters – the Foundation Years team has converted the booklet, poster and the cards from the Birth to Three Matters packs into PDFs for practitioners to download: http://www.foundationyears.org.uk/wp-content/uploads/2012/04/Birth-to-Three-Matter-Cards.pdf

Development Matters in the Early Years Foundation Stage (EYFS) – this non-statutory guidance material supports practitioners in implementing the statutory requirements of the EYFS. It includes useful charts on 'observing what a child is learning', covering each aspect of the seven learning areas for each age range: birth to 11 months; 8 to 20 months; 16 to 26 months; 22 to 36 months. Note this important reminder included at the bottom of each page:

> 'Children develop at their own rates, and in their own ways. The development statements and their order should not be taken as necessary steps for individual children. They should not be used as checklists. The age/stage bands overlap because these are not fixed age boundaries but suggest a typical range of development.'

2013 Early Years Foundation Stage Handbook – contains detailed information about EYFS assessments and guidance on how to complete the EYFS Profile. The Handbook should be used alongside the EYFS Profile exemplification materials; both available from the DfE: http://www.education.gov.uk/schools/teachingandlearning/assessment/eyfs/a00217599/eyfs-handbook

Early Education – this website provides access to the non-statutory guidance Development Matters in the Early Years Foundation Stage (EYFS) to support practitioners in implementing the statutory requirements of the EYFS – visit: http://www.early-education.org.uk/sites/default/files/Development%20Matters%20FINAL%20PRINT%20AMENDED.pdf

Early Years Experience – this website provides ideas, resources and information for practitioners, parents and carers of preschool, nursery and Key Stage 1 children (5 to 7 years of age): http://www.bigeyedowl.co.uk/index.htm

Early Years Matters – this website has a useful section: Observation, Assessment and Planning: http://earlyyearsmatters.co.uk/index.php/planning/

Foundation Years – this website (developed by 4Children) is the 'one stop shop' for resources, information and the latest news on the foundation years. The website provides advice and guidance for practitioners on working effectively with parents as partners in their children's learning: http://www.foundationyears.org.uk/

Know How Guide – The EYFS Progress Check at Age Two (2012) – this non-statutory guidance produced by the National Children's Bureau and supported by the DfE is intended to support practitioners in implementing the EYFS Progress Check at Age Two. Available at: https://www.education.gov.uk/publications/eOrderingDownload/EYFS%20-%20know%20how%20materials.pdf

New Childcare – this website (designed to help childcare students) includes useful information on: observing child development; improving observation skills for childcare students; development profiles: http://www.newchildcare.co.uk/

Principles for engaging with families – this framework for local authorities and national organisations to evaluate and improve engagement with families, produced by the Early Learning Partnership Engagement Group, is a free, downloadable resource available at: http://staging.ncb. baigentpreview.com/media/236258/engaging_with_families.pdf

Teaching Expertise – this website contains free topical teaching inspiration, ideas and recommendations, including a section with articles relating to the Early Years: http://www. teachingexpertise.com/topic/early-years

Books and articles

Abbott, L. and **Langston**, A. (2005) *Birth to Three Matters: Supporting the Framework of Effective Practice.* Milton Keynes: Open University Press.

Alcott, M. (2002) *An Introduction to Children with Special Needs*. London: Hodder & Stoughton.

ATL (2010) *Achievement for All: Working with Children with Special Educational Needs in Mainstream Schools and Colleges*. 3rd Edition. Association of Teachers and Lecturers. PDF available free from: http://www.atl.org.uk/Images/Achievment%20for%20all%20(2010).pdf

Barber, J. and **Paul-Smith**, S. (2012) *Early Years Observation and Planning in Practice: Your Guide to Best Practice and Use of Different Methods for Planning and Observation in the EYFS*. 2nd Edition. Salisbury: Practical Pre-School Books.

Beeley, K. (2012) *Science in the Early Years: How to Make Science Integral to Children's Learning*. Lutterworth: Featherstone Education.

Bertram, T. and **Pascal**, C. (2012) *The Revised Early Years Foundation Stage Curriculum: Implications for Practice*. Birmingham: Centre for Research in Early Childhood.

Bogas, P. (2011) *How to Do a Format Anecdote for Preschool.* http://www.ehow.com/how_12205700_format-anecdote-preschool.html#ixzz26ICBmDK (accessed October 2012).

Bruce, T. (2011) *Learning Through Play: For Babies, Toddlers and Young Children*. 2nd Edition. London: Hodder Education.

Bryson, S. (2007) 'Listening to the views of very young children'. This *Early Years Update* article is from September 2007. http://www.teachingexpertise.com/articles/listening-to-the-views-of-very-young-children-2500 (accessed September 2012).

Clarke, J. (2008) 'Fostering thinking skills in early years'. This *Early Years Update* article is from June 2008. http://www.teachingexpertise.com/articles/fostering-thinking-skills-early-years-3914 (accessed September 2012).

Cleaver, H. *et al*. (2009) *Safeguarding Children: A Shared Responsibility*. Chichester: Wiley-Blackwell.

Coleman, C. (2012) *What Is an Observation Schedule?* http://www.ehow.com/facts_7774047_observation-schedule.html#ixzz28FfXqlwp (accessed October 2012).

Dare, A. and **O'Donovan**, M. (2009) *Good Practice in Caring for Children with Special Needs*. 3rd Edition. Cheltenham: Nelson Thornes.

DCSF (2008a) *Information Sharing: Guidance for Practitioners and Managers.* DCSF & Communities and Local Government. https://www.education.gov.uk/publications/eOrderingDownload/00807-2008BKT-EN-March09.pdf

DCSF (2008b) *Information Sharing: Further Guidance on Legal Issues*. https://www.education.gov.uk/publications/standard/Integratedworking/Page1/DCSF-00857-2008

DCSF (2009) *Progress Matters: Reviewing and Enhancing Young Children's Development.* Department for Children, Schools and Families. http://www.foundationyears.org.uk/2012/05/progress-matters-reviewing-and-enhancing-young-childrens-development

DCSF/QCDA (2009) *Learning, Playing and Interacting: Good Practice in the Early Years Foundation Stage.* Department for Children, Schools and Families. http://earlylearningconsultancy.co.uk/wp-content/uploads/2011/02/Learning-Playing-and-Interacting.-final1.pdf

DCSF (2010) *Working Together to Safeguard Children: A Guide to Inter-agency Working to Safeguard and Promote the Welfare of Children*. https://www.education.gov.uk/publications/eOrderingDownload/00305-2010DOM-EN.pdf

DfE (2007) *The Early Years Foundation Stage – Effective Practice: Observation, Assessment and Planning*. Department for Education. http://www.bristol.gov.uk/sites/default/files/assets/documents/childminding-ofsted-effective-practice.pdf

DfE (2008) *Social and Emotional Aspects of Development: Guidance for Practitioners in the Early Years Foundation Stage.* https://www.education.gov.uk/publications/standard/EarlyYearseducationandchildcare/Page6/DCSF-00707-2008

DfE (2011a) *Information Sharing: How to Share Information Securely*. Department for Education. http://media.education.gov.uk/assets/files/pdf/h/how%20to%20share%20information%20securely.pdf

DfE (2011b) *Statutory Framework for the Early Years Foundation Stage: Setting the Standards for Learning, Development and Care for Children from Birth to Five. Draft for Consultation, 6 July 2011*. Department for Education. http://kathybigio.com/pdf/revised_early_years_foundation_stage.pdf

DfE (2011c) *Reforming the Early Years Foundation Stage (the EYFS): Government Response to Consultation 20 December 2011.* Department for Education. http://www.education.gov.uk/consultations/downloadableDocs/Government%20response%20doc%20191211%201630%20finaltext%20KM%20CB%201808(v2).pdf

DfE (2012) *Statutory Framework for the Early Years Foundation Stage: Setting the Standards for Learning, Development and Care for Children from Birth to Five*. Department for Education. https://www.education.gov.uk/publications/eOrderingDownload/EYFS%20Statutory%20Framework%20March%202012.pdf

DfES (2001) *The Special Educational Needs Code of Practice 2001*. HMSO. https://www.education.gov.uk/publications/standard/publicationDetail/Page1/DfES%200581%202001

Digman, C. and **Soan**, S. (2008) *Working with Parents: A Guide for Educational Professionals*. London: Sage Publications.

DoH, **DfE** and the **Home Office** (2000) *Framework for the Assessment of Children in Need and Their Families*. HMSO.

Dubiel, J. (2008) 'What's the point of early years assessment?' This *Early Years Update* article is from July 2008. http://www.teachingexpertise.com/articles/what%E2%80%99s-point-early-years-assessment-4053 (accessed September 2012).

Early Education (2012) *Development Matters in the Early Years Foundation Stage (EYFS).* Non-statutory guidance to support practitioners in implementing the statutory requirements of the EYFS. http://www.early-education.org.uk/sites/default/files/Development%20Matters%20FINAL%20 PRINT%20AMENDED.pdf (accessed September 2012).

Elfer, P. (2005) 'Observation Matters' (see Abbott and Langston, 2005).

Erwin, L and **Sanderson**, H. (2010) *One-page Profiles with Children and Young People*. HSA Press. http://www.helensandersonassociates.co.uk/media/38428/onepageprofilesinschools.pdf (accessed September 2012).

EYM (2012) *Observation, Assessment and Planning*. Early Years Matters website: http://earlyyearsmatters.co.uk/index.php/planning/ (accessed September 2012).

EYU (2008) 'Early years: eight principles for observational assessment'. This *Early Years Update* article is from April 2008. http://www.teachingexpertise.com/articles/early-years-eight-principles-for-observational-assessment-3355 (accessed September 2012).

Fiore, L.B. (2012) *Assessment of Young Children: A Collaborative Approach*. Oxford: Routledge.

Fisher, J. (2010) *Moving on to Key Stage 1: Improving Transition from the Early Years Foundation Stage*. Milton Keynes: Open University Press.

Gallow, C. (2012) *Trackers: Tracking children's progress through the Early Years Foundation Stage*. Stafford: QEd Publications: www.qed.uk.com

Gascoyne, S. (2012) *Treasure Baskets and Beyond: Realizing the Potential of Sensory-rich Play*. Milton Keynes: Open University Press.

Gatiss, S. (1991) '5. Parents as Partners' in *Signposts to Special Needs: An Information Pack on Meeting Special Educational Needs in the Mainstream Classroom*. London: National Children's Bureau and NES Arnold.

Gillespie-Edwards, A. (2002) *Relationships and Learning: Caring for Children from Birth to Three*. London: National Children's Bureau.

Harding, J. (2013) *Child Development: An Illustrated Handbook*. London: Hodder Education.

Harding, J. and **Meldon-Smith**, L. (2001) *How to Make Observations and Assessments*. 2nd Edition. London: Hodder & Stoughton.

Harvey, N. (2006) *Effective Communication*. 2nd Revised Edition. Dublin: Gill & MacMillan Ltd.

Hobart, C. and **Frankel**, J. (2005) *A Practical Guide to Activities for Young Children*. 3rd Edition. Cheltenham: Nelson Thornes.

Horwath, J. (2001) *The Child's World: Assessing Children in Need*. London: Jessica Kingsley Publishers.

Hughes, A. (2010) *Developing Play for the Under 3s: The Treasure Basket and Heuristic Play*. Oxford: Routledge.

Hutchin, V. (1999) *Right from the Start: Effective Planning and Assessment in the Early Years*. London: Hodder & Stoughton.

Hutchin, V. (2012) *Assessing and Supporting Young Children's Learning for the Early Years Foundation Stage Profile*. London: Hodder Education.

Hutchin, V. (2012) *The EYFS: A Practical Guide for Students and Professionals*. London: Hodder Education.

ICO (2012) *The Data Protection Act – Your Responsibilities and Obligations to Data Protection*. Information Commissioner's Office: www.ico.gov.uk/what_we_cover/data_protection.aspx

Jaeckle, S. (2008) 'The EYFS principles: a breakdown'. This *Early Years Update* article is from September 2008. http://www.teachingexpertise.com/articles/eyfs-principles-breakdown-4117 (accessed February 2012).

Kagan, S.L., **Shepard**, L. and **Wurtz**, E. (eds) (1998) *Principles and Recommendations for Early Childhood Assessments.* National Education Goals Panel. http://govinfo.library.unt.edu/negp/reports/prinrec.pdf (accessed October 2012).

Kamen, T. (2000) *Psychology for Childhood Studies*. London: Hodder & Stoughton.

Kamen, T. (2011) *Teaching Assistant's Handbook Level 3: Supporting Teaching and Learning in Schools*. London: Hodder Education.

Katz, L.G. (1997) *A Developmental Approach to Assessment of Young Children*. ERIC Digest. http://www.eric.ed.gov/PDFS/ED407172.pdf (accessed October 2012).

Le Page, K. (2010a) *Observation Methods for Assessing Child Development.* Suite 101 website: http://suite101.com/article/observation-methods-for-assessing-child-development-a242883 (accessed October 2012).

Le Page, K. (2010b) *Understanding Child Observation Methods.* Suite 101 website: http://suite101.com/article/understanding-child-observation-methods-a242958 (accessed October 2012).

Limbrick-Spencer, G. (2001) *The Keyworker: A Practical Guide*. Birmingham: WordWorks.

Lindon, L. (2002) *Good Practice in Working with Babies, Toddlers and Very Young Children*. London: SureStart.

Lindon, J. (2012a) *Safeguarding and Child Protection 0–8 Years*. 4th Edition. London: Hodder Education.

Lindon, J. (2012b) *Equality and Inclusion in Early Childhood*. 2nd Edition. London: Hodder Education.

Lindon, J. (2012c) *Understanding Child Development 0–11 Years*. London: Hodder Education.

Meggitt, C. (2012) *Child Development: An Illustrated Guide*. 3rd Edition with DVD. London: Pearson Education.

Meggitt, C., **Kamen**, T., **Bruce**, T. and **Grenier**, J. (2011) *CACHE Level 3 Diploma: Children and Young People's Workforce – Early Learning and Child Care*. London: Hodder Education.

Miller, L. (2002) *Observation Observed: An Outline of the Nature and Practice of Infant Observation*. London: Tavistock Clinic Foundation.

Miller, L., **Cable**, C. and **Devereux**, J. (2005) *Developing Early Years Practice*. London: David Fulton Publishers.

Morrison, G.R. (2007) *Fundamentals of Early Childhood Education*. 5th Edition. New Jersey: Prentice Hall.

Mortimer, H. (2008) *Playladders*. Stafford: QEd Publications: www.qed.uk.com

Mortimer, H. (2001) *Special Needs and Early Years Provision*. London: Continuum International Publishing Group Ltd.

NCB (2012) *A Know How Guide: The EYFS Progress Check at Age Two.* National Children's Bureau. http://www.foundationyears.org.uk/wp-content/uploads/2012/03/A-Know-How-Guide.pdf

Neaum, S. (2010) *Child Development for Early Childhood Studies*. Exeter: Learning Matters.

NSPCC (2010) *Child Abuse Reporting Requirements for Professionals*. NSPCC factsheet: http://www.nspcc.org.uk/Inform/research/questions/reporting_child_abuse_wda74908.html

O'Brien, A. (2005) 'Assessment for learning: a key skill'. This *Early Years Update* article is from December 2005. http://www.teachingexpertise.com/articles/assessment-for-learning-a-key-skill-1144 (accessed October 2012).

O'Toole, A. (2002) *Assessing Young Learners.* http://www.countryschool.com/ylsig/members/summaries/assessing.htm (accessed October 2012).

Palaiologou, I. (2012) *Child Observation for the Early Years*. 2nd Edition. Exeter: Learning Matters.

Ragg, R. (2010) 'EYFS: Observation Tips' in *Early Years* spring 2010. https://www.education.gov.uk/publications/eOrderingDownload/DCSF-00137-2010.pdf (accessed September 2012).

Ramsey, R. (2002) *How to Say the Right Thing Every Time: Communicating Well with Students, Staff, Parents and the Public*. London: Corwin Press.

Sanderson, H., **Smith**, T. and **Wilson**, L. (2010) *One Page Profiles in Schools – A Guide*. HSA Press. http://www.helensandersonassociates.co.uk/media/38450/oppinschlguide.pdf (accessed December 2012).

Seitz, H. and **Bartholomew**, C. (2008) 'Powerful Portfolios for Young Children' in *Early Childhood Education Journal.* Springer Science+Business Media. Published online 29.03.08. http://sttechnology.pbworks.com/f/Seitz_(2008)_Powerful%20Portfolios%20for%20Young%20Children.pdf (accessed November 2012).

Sheridan, M., **Sharma**, A. and **Cockerill**, H. (2007) *From Birth to Five Years: Children's Developmental Progress*. 3rd Edition. Oxford: Routledge.

Smidt, S. (2005) *Observing, Assessing and Planning for Children in the Early Years*. Oxford: Routledge.

Smith, M., **Kamen**, T., **Irvine**, J., **Armitage**, M. and **Barker**, C. (2012) *CACHE Level 3 Extended Diploma: Children and Young People's Workforce – Early Learning and Child Care*. London: Hodder Education.

Stewart, N. (2011) *How Children Learn: The Characteristics of Effective Early Learning*. London: Early Education.

Thornton, L. and **Brunton**, P. (2010a) 'The value of play in early years'. This *Early Years Update* article is from January 2010. http://www.teachingexpertise.com/e-bulletins/value-play-early-years-7814 (accessed September 2012).

Thornton, L. and **Brunton**, P. (2010b) 'Accelerate learning in early years using Treasure Baskets'. This *Early Years Update* article is from March 2010. http://www.teachingexpertise.com/e-bulletins/accelerate-learning-early-years-using-treasure-baskets-8030 (accessed October 2012).

Tickell, C. (2011) *The Early Years: Foundations for Life, Health and Learning – An Independent Report on the Early Years Foundation Stage to Her Majesty's Government*. http://media.education. gov.uk/assets/files/pdf/f/the%20early%20years%20foundations%20for%20life%20health%20 and%20learning.pdf

Wall, K. (2006) *Special Needs & Early Years: A Practitioner's Guide*. 2nd Edition. London: Sage Publications Ltd. Chapter 5 available online: http://www.sagepub.com/upm-data/9656_022816Ch5. pdf

Index